Seized

FOR HIS GLORY

Seized

FOR HIS
GLORY

Brenda J. Robinson

WINEPRESS WP PUBLISHING

Printed in the United States of America

Cover design: Ragont Design

Packaged by WinePress Publishing, PO Box 428, Enumclaw, WA 98022. The views expressed or implied in this work do not necessarily reflect those of WinePress Publishing. The author(s) is ultimately responsible for the design, content, and editorial accuracy of this work.

Unless otherwise noted, all scriptures are taken from the King James Version of the Bible.

ISBN 1-57921-458-4
Library of Congress Catalog Card Number: 2002103348

This book is lovingly dedicated to my son, Labron, for giving me a reason to keep going when life seemed hopeless, for always knowing that God was in control, and for being a constant reminder that life, no matter how bad it seems, is nothing to get stressed out over.

I would also like to dedicate this book to the memory of my dear mother, Lola Holcombe, who taught me about God and His love every day. It was her words of God's love and righteousness that came back to my remembrance and helped bring me back to a victorious walk with Him.

Contents

Acknowledgements

*S*pecial thanks to my husband, Dan, who faithfully supports my ministry and makes the necessary sacrifices to see that I can do what God has called me to do. Your understanding, love, and patience is appreciated more than words can say. Thank you for the words of encouragement that give me the strength to go on when I feel like giving up.

I also want to give special thanks to my sisters, Dolly and Debra, who stood faithfully by my side for six long and painful years of sickness and despair. I know that we could not have made it through that time if the two of you hadn't been there. Thanks for all you've done and all that you continue to do. I love you both dearly.

An overwhelming thanks goes to my two boys, Kevin and Labron, who made my heart smile when I couldn't find anything to smile about. You both are my sunshine.

Last, but not least, my greatest appreciation can go to none other than my personal assistant and my friend, Karen Tinsley, who has so patiently and professionally made this book what it is today. Thank you, Karen.

Foreword

*E*pilepsy is a disorder that can affect different people in different ways. So, telling you that Brenda Robinson had epilepsy won't really tell you how it affected *her* or *her family*. Epilepsy is also a widely misunderstood illness—one often shrouded in fear, pain, and misplaced shame.

To me epilepsy was, plain and simple, a disorder that caused seizures. I thought the only thing that made an epileptic different from me was the fact that they couldn't, or shouldn't, drive a car. Besides Brenda, I have known one other person with epilepsy, though in ten years I never knew him to have a seizure or to show the visible aftereffects of one. In my mind, epilepsy affected everyone in the same way. In reality, it does not.

Through the course of this writing, I studied epilepsy in-depth. I found many of the facts very interesting—if not unbelievable.

Throughout her story, you will read various accounts of Brenda's seizures and her response to their arresting hold. But the bare facts about seizures and the disorder of epilepsy given here may help you to comprehend even more fully the disabling grip of the disease on the lives of its sufferers and those who love them:

Facts About Epilepsy

Epilepsy is a brain disorder that interrupts normal electrical brain activity.

Epilepsy is characterized by many symptoms including:
- uncontrolled body movements
- disorientation or confusion
- sudden fear
- loss of consciousness.

No cause for epilepsy is found in nearly 70% of cases.

Seizures vary in intensity and symptoms depending on the part of the brain involved. Some cause sight or hearing impairment, and feelings of fear.

Others cause the victim to appear to be in a trance or to display random and illogical behavior. Some seizures are preceded by an aura (a "mental" warning that the seizure is coming on). Still other seizures cause a temporary loss of consciousness with the victim often unaware of the onset. *Grand mal* seizures are characterized by jerking muscular contractions which affect the entire body. Afterwards, the patient is exhausted and usually sleeps deeply. However, the patient often has no recollection of the seizure upon regaining consciousness, although he may suffer nausea, confusion and sore muscles. In rare cases, the patient may seize successively with no intervening periods of consciousness, which may be fatal.

There is no cure for epilepsy, Only the symptoms can be treated.

As you read on in this book, please keep one fact about epilepsy especially in mind: "There is no cure for epilepsy." This is an undisputed medical fact. I'll never forget the first time I heard Dan share his testimony about the struggles that he and Brenda went through for six years battling the baffling disease of epilepsy. He said, "We had to take our eyes off the healing and put them on the Healer." While there may not be a cure for epilepsy, I'm glad there is a Healer!

In Christ,
Karen Tinsley, personal assistant to Brenda Robinson
New Desire Christian Ministries, Inc.
Aragon, Georgia

Foreword

For several years I have been intrigued by the servanthood of Dr. Brenda Robinson. Her love for Christ and His work, her knowledge of God's Word, and her wisdom in applying the precepts of the Word are all very apparent in her personal and professional life. Her in-depth Bible study is also visible in her teachings, her writings, and her manner of fulfilling the many administrative responsibilities of coordinating staff schedules for the outreach programs of New Desire Ministries.

Brenda's writings, speaking messages, individual and group counseling lessons have ministered to thousands of hurting individuals. She has written commentaries and dealt with hundreds of practical Bible topics that concern practicing Christians today. I believe she possesses one of the most powerful pens in the twenty-first century, and I anticipate God using Dr. Robinson to produce spiritual fruit in the lives of all who will be nourished by it far beyond anything she has ever imagined or dreamed.

I am sure you will find this writing to be in harmony with the infallible and inherent Word of God. Dr. Robinson has a unique way of educating and encouraging the Christian in a fashion that is easily understood and applied. Her goals for writing are clearly twofold; first, to lead the lost to the Lord Jesus Christ; and secondly, to teach believers more about their Lord. Whatever your need may be today, you can use this reading to come to a saving knowledge of Jesus Christ and/or to enhance your own spiritual growth.

I'm convinced that Dr. Robinson does not write to place herself in the spotlight, *nor* to become a famous writer, *nor* to draw attention to herself. No, quite honestly, it is this kind of thinking that repulses her most. Dr. Robinson does not write to *get*, but to give. She writes to serve, not to be served, and to bring honor and glory to the Lamb of God.

Drawn from her own life's struggles and journey, Dr. Robinson's devotional insights are warm and spiritually priceless. As you will discover, she has persevered through many struggles—including severe medical problems, the financial stress of tremendous medical bills, and the shadows of her own past—in pursuit of the high calling that God placed on her life.

I have known Dr. Robinson to keep her scheduled appointments even when she had to depend on her husband and family to dress her because she was not able to do it for herself. She would literally have to be carried into the facility where she was scheduled to appear. During the very intense times of her seizures, when she was bedridden and so ill she was unable to perform the daily activities of living, Dr. Robinson, like Mary, chose the better part—to sit at Jesus' feet. It is this determination that allowed her to learn more about Jesus so that others could one day be taught of Him. She is therefore well equipped to share the truth that, regardless of adversities, one can continue to grow spiritually in Christ if one exercises the desire to do so.

You have in your possession a book penned from the heart, ordained and anointed by God. You have an instrument that will guide you into a deeper understanding of and a richer walk with God. Through Dr. Robinson's many labors and her choice to persevere in Christ, this book is now yours. Yet in the final analysis each reader must read, study, and carefully practice the godly principles she has presented. And it is God who will hold each of us responsible for our application of the Christian faith and principles this courageous woman's life reflects.

Barry Keaton, Ph.D.
Pastor, Holly Springs Baptist Church and author of *Country Counseling*
Founder and CEO, Comfort Care Ministries, Inc.
Affiliate, West Georgia Counseling and Educational Services

Foreword

*G*od had been breathing new life into the Ladies Sunday School class I co-taught at West Metro Baptist Church with my dear friend, Nancy Dempsey. For one thing, He'd brought twenty-five-year-old Suzanna Ray into our class, and she was generously bestowing her twin gifts of encouragement and hospitality upon our entire class of forty and fifty-something saints. Suzanna regularly sent us each sweet little notes reminding us she was thinking of and praying for us. Then she began organizing fellowship events for the class. She took us to a Twila Paris concert in October and made us a beautiful Christmas dinner in December.

One day in late January Suzanna arrived in class with this "brilliant" idea to go to a Ladies event at Pumpkinvine Baptist Church. The event featured a luncheon and a guest speaker named Brenda Robinson. I was less than thrilled. Also, I thought I might know this Brenda Robinson. After class I asked Suzanna if this woman might be from anywhere near Paulding County, where we lived, or if she was an outside speaker that Pumpkinvine was bringing in for the upcoming event. Suzanna said she'd check into it.

A week later, Suzanna came back to report that, yes, Brenda Robinson was a local speaker, but she was unable to find out what she was going to speak about. I searched through the archives of my mind for a clearer memory of this woman. It had been many years, but I was pretty certain I had treated a patient named Brenda Robinson in my chiropractic office. It had been so long that I did not remember what I had treated her for, but I remembered her being pretty pathetic. I was certain the Brenda Robinson *I* vaguely recalled couldn't possibly have *anything* of any benefit to say to any one of us. I wasn't remembering a victorious child of the King, but a defeated one. I went to hear her mostly out of curiosity.

As she began to share the testimony of having suffered for six years with *grand mal* epileptic seizures that left her without speech and paralyzed on her right side, it all came back to me. After fifteen plus years, you might forget a face that was one of hundreds you'd seen that year, but you don't forget a story like that. I remembered that this woman was unable to speak, drive, care for herself, or even walk unassisted. Her sister Debra brought her to her appointments and spoke for her. I think there was even some left-handed note-writing when Debra didn't know the answer to a question.

I couldn't help but think that the ladies Brenda was speaking to at Pumpkinvine that morning were probably having a hard time believing someone as healthy and beautiful as Brenda could ever have been in the condition she was now describing (in vivid detail) to us. I can tell you that she was! Her miraculous healing probably sounded just too unbelievable to some. I, on the other hand, was having a hard time comprehending that this was really the woman I remembered. Her name and the incredible story were the same, but there was nothing about her appearance now that was even remotely similar!

I once heard of a special pottery that is made by taking the finished product and smashing it into pieces—to the horror of all bystanders. In this process, the potter then gingerly puts the pieces back together using fine gold as the "glue." The end product is more beautiful than it was before because the gold is intermingled throughout the fine ceramic piece like beautiful, strong lace.

The beauty of Brenda's life is not just that God healed her physically. As long as we live in this earth-suit, we will *all* have health issues from time to time. Brenda, like the rest of us, is not without the occasional health challenge herself, even today. The beauty, though, is what Jesus has done to her heart, and that through this she has learned to be content in Him no matter what her circumstances.

I was wrong to think that the speaker at Pumpkinvine would have nothing special to share with us that day. To my surprise, I saw a broken vessel who'd been lovingly and beautifully put back together by the Master—with gold "lace" shot through the clay of her small, human frame. Lord, forgive me, and glory to God for the victory Brenda walks in today! Oh, what a Savior we have!

Janet Haberer, D.C.
February 22, 2002
Paulding County, Georgia

Introduction
From a Distance

It was May, 1985. My husband Dan and I were returning from a wonderful weekend getaway in the mountains to our home in tiny Aragon, Georgia. My sister Debra, who lived close by, had invited us to dinner at her house that evening, and it was an offer I couldn't refuse.

The trip had been refreshing, but it had also been exhausting. To top it off, the whirlwind weekend was culminating in a throbbing headache. By the time we arrived at Debra's the headache was almost unbearable. As we sat down at the table for dinner, I hoped the delicious meal she'd prepared us would help relieve the pain until I could get home to rest. *Too much fun* had not been good for me.

Suddenly I found myself awaking in my sister's recliner—unsure what was going on. My body hurt all over, and everyone was waiting on me hand and foot. I thought maybe we were going somewhere, but I didn't know where or why. The last thing I'd remembered was sitting down to the supper table. Now I was sitting in the recliner—at the center of the family's attention.

I questioned Debra about the situation, and fear gripped me as she began to explain. "It's been two weeks since you sat down at that table," she said. In that space of time, she further explained, I had been through multiple . . . probably hundreds . . . of seizures. In the past two weeks, I had been from doctors' offices to hospitals, yet I had no recollection of any of it.

I soon began to realize that I also had no control of my body. Rather than doing what *I* told it to do, my body would curl up, jerk, and shake. The pain I felt was unbearable. My mind began to race. What had gone on for the last two weeks? I was still at Debra's house! Had I not even been home in that long? What about my children? Who was taking care of them? What had we done about food and clothing? I didn't even know if I had been conscious or unconscious for the past two weeks!

Wondering who had taken care of my family and what they had been doing during this time was hard. Mother had taught me that a woman was responsible for taking care of her husband and children, and now mine were being forced to take care of me. I couldn't even recall where I had been or what I had done for the previous fourteen days. I certainly didn't know how my family had managed to get by without me!

As I lay coiled in the fetal position in my sister's recliner, these and similar thoughts completely devastated me. My body was partially paralyzed and unable to function. My memory was gone. Two weeks of my life had been completely wiped out. I had to be cared for like an invalid. I could not even feed, clothe, or bathe myself. Unable to control my body, I had to be carried like a child just to go from one room to another.

Horrified, I couldn't understand what was happening or why. Just when Dan and I had thought that everything was going to be OK with our marriage and family, *this* had to happen. Fear gripped me. I began to go over my life, trying to find a reason for this catastrophic illness. Sitting in Debra's recliner that day, I slowly relived every moment from my childhood to that very moment—searching desperately through the details of my life for an answer to the question, *"Why? Why is this happening to me now?"* The video replay of my life looked something like the following . . .

Play it again, Ma'am

I was the baby of nine children. There were seven girls and two boys. Our father was an alcoholic. Most of the time, he lived in his own distant world. Our mother, on the other hand, was an extraordinary, hands-on woman. She worked as many jobs as necessary to provide for her family, and she taught us the love of God every day of our lives. We never had much materially. Mother raised all nine of her children in a twenty by thirty foot block home, but she made sure that we had a wealth of love.

At the age of twelve I took my first public job waiting tables after school. Mother taught us to work hard and to be responsible about everything in life. She also taught us to be independent and mature. Like everyone else, I had fallen short in some of these areas, but I knew that I had done the best I could.

For the most part, my teenage years were the typical roller coaster ride physically, mentally, and emotionally. There were many broken relationships: "boy meets girl, but things just don't work out quite as planned." I *was* more mature, however, than most people my age. By the age of fourteen, I was running our household on my own. Still, I had the usual teenage dreams of a better life built around a fabulous career. My dream was to become an airline stewardess. Boy, did I miss that one. The closest I've ever come to being an airline hostess is telling my children to fasten their seat belts!

At the age of sixteen, I left home looking for the *better life* I had dreamed of so often. From that time until I married Dan, my life was a string of broken relationships, including one broken marriage. By nineteen, I was a single parent . . . and miserable. I had gradually slipped away from the Christian standards that my mother had instilled within me, adopting the philosophy of "Eat, drink, and be merry, for tomorrow we die." This had not brought me the merriment expected . . .

Back to My Future

Curled up there in Debra's armchair, I knew I wasn't where I needed to be with God, but was that sufficient reason for Him to punish me with seizures? Sure, I wasn't perfect, but who was? Maybe I did have a social drink every now and then, but I had never committed murder or anything like that. No, there was *no* major sin in my life that could justify such punishment! I became furious with God.

God's and my views of sin just didn't match up, I figured. The things I was guilty of were just part of everyday life. A *loving* God would never view them as sins worthy of His severe judgment, yet I decided that this was just what I was facing. If this was God's cruel judgment on my life, I neither understood it nor liked it.

In the days following this first bout with epileptic seizures, I grew even more bitter and angry with God. I didn't want any part of the Christian life. I didn't want people to even *talk* about God around me. I viewed Him as cruel and unloving. Every experience with God that I could recall was painful and bitter, and I could think of at least *a dozen* other people who deserved this kind of punishment much more than I did. Yet the more bitter I became, the worse my physical situation grew.

Within two years, I'd hit rock bottom. The doctors gave me no hope. In fact, they gave me only five years to live. My seizures were now coming on so hard that the doctor fully expected me to have a massive heart attack and die during one of them. I would realize then that I had nowhere to turn but to God.

God at Work

Meanwhile, I continued watching the "instant replay" of my life. Everything that my mother had taught me about God was now coming back to my remembrance. I remembered how she would put us on the church bus and send us to Sunday School, and the things that I had learned about Him there were precious. I remembered learning that God was not cruel and punishing, but that He was full of love, grace, forgiveness, and mercy. I suddenly realized that I had been analyzing God's actions rather than experiencing Him in my circumstances. And I'd *refused* to learn what He'd wanted so desperately to teach me about Himself. That's when I began to search for *God at work* in my life—even in the grip of epilepsy.

Chapter 1

The Search

The search for God in my life would have to begin with a search through my childhood. If I could see His hand at work there, then surely I would see how He had been working in my life all along. You see, childhood was a time of great emotional strain for me. In the small, rural town of Dallas, Georgia, about an hour west of Atlanta, there were only two kinds of people: saints and sinners—and my parents represented the furthest extremes of each! Balancing ourselves between want and plenty, the sacred and the profane, desire and disgust could sometimes lead to inner and outer tensions that bordered on the dysfunctional . . . if not outright defined it!

Beyond his frequent drinking, my father became very abusive when drunk. There were many, many nights when I would lie on my top bunk praying fervently that my father would not hurt my mother. Because she would not allow him to beat us, dad beat my mother. She, on the other hand, was always loving and patient. Many times we children would question her determination to stay with our father in spite of his abusiveness, but she always responded in the same way. "If we don't love him with God's love, no one else will. It is our responsibility to show him Jesus."

There were many times when mom would force dad to leave the home, or for our safety she would gather all of us children up and leave. But dad would always sober up eventually, and the family would be reunited. My mother continued to live like this for forty-two years, refusing to leave my father or to break our family apart. Finally, when all of her children were grown, she separated permanently from dad. Although she never divorced, mom refused to live under the same roof with him in those circumstances again.

Believe it or not, my father was the nicest man in the world when he was sober, but alcohol brought out the beast in him. He didn't feel responsible to provide for his family, either. In his mind, my father's money was *his* money. He used it any way he wanted, regardless of what the family wanted or needed. Truthfully, I cannot remember my father ever buying me a single pair of shoes. Mother worked two or three jobs at a time just to feed, clothe, and send us to school. Though she could not depend on my father for *anything*, she never complained. She just did what she had to do to make sure that we had what we needed.

Fire!

The most memorable day in my early childhood took place when I was just six years old. Mother called the school one day and left a message for us to catch the bus to her father's house, where she would pick us up that afternoon. When we stepped off the school bus at our grandfather's house, mother sat us down to tell us that our home had burned to the ground. She told us that we would have to live with our grandfather until we could get back on our feet.

With the little money she received from the homeowner's insurance, mother built a twenty by thirty foot block basement for our new home. When the basement was completed, we moved in. Soon after, mother soon became very sick, and we were unable to finish building our new home. With little other option besides, Mother raised all nine of us in that twenty by thirty foot block basement. We didn't have a lot of room, but we always had each other, and we always had love.

Can you imagine what it would be like to live in a twenty by thirty foot block building with nine kids and an unstable spouse? People were fascinated to see how we even lived and slept. Our home looked like a Marine barracks. There were bunk beds stacked on top of bunk beds. Most of the time, we slept two to a bunk, one at the head and one at the foot. We had such close quarters that when one person forgot to take a bath, everybody else knew it!

In spite of how little we had, mother never complained. She was always thankful for what she did have, and she taught us to appreciate *everything* in life. She never allowed herself to dwell on the negative. My father was just the opposite. He lived in his own little world—and never found a positive thing to say about it!

Growing, Growing, Grown . . .

Mother's illness gradually became worse, and by the time I was twelve years old I'd been taken out of school to help take care of her. Daddy was still coming, going, and spending his money however he wanted to. My brother Dennis and I were, by this time, the only ones left at home. Dennis worked a job at a carpet mill to help provide for us when father was away. We used his check, mother's disability, and the little money that others gave us to pay the bills and buy just enough groceries to feed ourselves.

As soon as I was old enough to move away from home, I did. I had grown weary of lying in bed wondering if I would find mother dead the next morning due to my dad's abuse during the night. By the time I was sixteen, my nerves were shot. I knew I had to go out and find a life of my own. I could not continue to live with the stress at home.

I guess watching my mother live in such an unstable and abusive relationship for so many years instilled within me a determination never to have this type of relationship with anyone. So I went from one imperfect relationship to another. I searched for love, peace, and happiness in all the wrong places. Though outwardly active and goal-oriented, I was the most insecure person you could ever meet.

When I made the decision to leave home, I also decided to live life the way I wanted. Although my mother had taught me about Jesus every day and sent me to church every week, when I left home I walked out on God, too. I had grown tired of classmates making fun of me at school because my clothes were not name brand. I was weary of feeling like I was *less than* others because we were poor and didn't have nice things. My mother had taught me to hold my head up and not fall prey to peer pressure, but I was tired of the negative, dog-eat-dog world I had been living in. I wanted a stress-free and more positive way of life. There had to be something better out there somewhere, I thought.

My search for a better life was not fun. In fact, the farther out into the world I went, the worse still life became. Yet for many years—convinced that I was making it on my own—I called this *fun* and happiness. I found a great job as a dance teacher, bought myself a car, made some new friends, and outfitted myself with some new clothes. Persuaded that I was living it up, I nearly killed myself trying to live up to everyone else's standards. I thought I had to have the nicest house and car and to wear the nicest clothes. I was so insecure with myself that I would do whatever it took to have friends. And the more *friends* I made, the more expenses I incurred. Then, when the expenses became more than I could handle and my money slowly dwindled away, my friends disappeared, too.

My fear of not being accepted by others made me a very emotionally unstable young woman. In fact, my life from ages sixteen to twenty became *very* unstable. My inferiority complex drove me to work hard to prove myself to others just to feel like I fit in. My insecurities and emotional instability brought on many broken relationships with men in my life. As is the case for so many young girls, my heart was broken over and over by men who I thought would respect me and accept me for who I was. It seems I always looked for love "in all the wrong places." This lifestyle went on for several years, and by the age of twenty I had already married and divorced, and I had a bouncing baby boy to raise all on my own.

As You Sow . . . *Reaping the Whirlwind*

During those years of *wilderness living* I was injured on my job. Stretching things more than I should have, I managed to injure my back pretty severely, but I did not pursue any type of compensation for the accident. I had been raised to understand that the Bible taught strictly against lawsuits, so I continued working in spite of severe back pain. Soon I began to experience paralysis and muscle spasms throughout my back, arms, and legs. The severity of these symptoms caused me to miss work for weeks at a time. Tests later showed that I had permanent disc, nerve, and muscle damage.

I was forced to change jobs and my income decreased drastically. On top of this, my determination to survive in life was slowly diminishing. I lived in excruciating pain everyday. The financial strain from my loss of work while trying to raise a child became more than I could bear. At the age of twenty-one, I had become very fragile mentally, physically, and emotionally. I felt like I was trapped in a dark hole with no way out.

In a world so full of people, I felt all alone. And the harder I fought to survive, the weaker I grew. I lay in bed at night and cried myself to sleep. I became depressed and lost an extreme amount of weight. Life had become nothing more than worry, stress, and fear. I believe now that the only thing that kept me going was my precious baby boy.

As the treasured days of Labron's first year of life were drawing to a close, I began searching for some kind of inner peace. Looking around, I had come to the realization that I had made a complete mess of my life. I had been trying to cover the guilt and shame of immature decisions with a *temporary fix* of material goods and *good times* that I had mistaken for true happiness. Now I was starting to reap exactly what I had sown: the whirlwind. I had sown to the flesh, and I was reaping the bad harvest.

My search for peace brought many of my mother's words back to my thoughts. Certain phrases that she'd used rang out constantly with particular poignancy to my now-listening ears. "You can't do anything without God," mother would say. *"Could she possibly have been right?"* I wondered. In my arrogance, it seemed impossible that that corny old phrase could hold the key to all truth for *me*. Yet every time I tried to make sense out of my life or find peace in my circumstance the words *"without God"* would come to my re-membrance.

And oh yes, I tried very vigorously to justify my lifestyle by telling myself that I was not such a bad person. There were lots of people doing worse things than I was! What about all those people who had committed murder or who'd had abortions? I hadn't done anything *that* bad. The worst thing I was guilty of was having a drink every now and then, but I had seen enough of the effects of alcohol in my father's life to avoid excesses in *that* area. I had always feared drugs and sex, so I'd stayed away from people involved in those activities.

In my eyes, I was *OK*. God didn't see me that way. In His eyes, sin is sin. There are no *big sins* and *little sins,* and He found me as guilty as the murderer, the abortionist, the drunk, and the prostitute. This "argument with God" about my supposed righteousness lasted for quite some time. Then somehow (whether through the Word, a message heard from the pulpit or in a still, small Voice that spoke to me within), my vain attempts to justify my lifestyle brought me face to face with the truth. I found true peace in God's truth, and my search ended in Him.

At last, though I had so long forgotten, it was becoming quite clear that God had been working in my life since as a young child I had received Him as my Savior.

Memories of Me

As the "videotape" of my childhood continued, I remembered that The Holy Spirit had convicted my heart of sin and of my need for Christ at a Tuesday night revival meeting. I had responded and received Jesus when I was twelve years old. I remembered again just how it felt when I first realized that God had chosen me to be His child and how His mercy and grace had protected me all the way through the rebellious years that started when I was sixteen.

Incredibly, I thought, God's plan for my life had been in place long before He'd saved me, and had unfolded in His perfect time. He knew all along what it would take to mold me and make me into His vessel. He had given me a mother who would teach me of His love and power. Then He'd used my mother to teach me that what I viewed as faults, failures, and mistakes could be made victorious lessons in my life if I would just give them to God.

I can sincerely say that the skeletons in my closet are now on display for the world to see. I am no longer ashamed, trapped, or controlled by my past or by my past failures. I voluntarily display everything about my life here with the hope that God's power and personhood will be seen through my experiences. If God could change my life as a result of my turning to Him (even though it took my coming to a place of great pain and humility to do it), I am certain that He can and will do the same for anyone else.

The times in which I felt abandoned by God the most, He was working on me. At twenty-one-years old, I wanted no part of God. I was living a life characterized by sin and rebellion, yet in His love God reached down and planted the man he had chosen for me right in the middle of it.

When Dan walked into my life, my search for a lasting and loving relationship was over. I had finally found someone who could love me and accept me just for who I was, but God still had a great deal of work to do in both of our lives. At that time, neither Dan nor I was active in church, in prayer, or in service to others. Ultimately, God would have to mold us into the image of His Son, Jesus Christ, in order to make our relationship work at all!

But the Lord was so kind and patient, allowing Dan and me to grow up together in Him. From the beginning of our relationship until this very day we have, by the grace of God, weathered many storms and traversed the heights and depths of God-ordained marital love. But that's another story . . .

In the Beginning

*I*n 1982 I was working at a local convenience store in Aragon as the evening sales clerk. My life consisted of little more than work and my son, Labron, who had just turned two.

Mother had taught all of us to make two sacrifices in life. The first was to put God first in everything; the second was to put our children before ourselves and our own desires. She had taught me that my children were *my* responsibility; therefore I spent almost all of my time off work with Labron. I tried desperately to be the same kind of mom that my mother had been, but I found that lofty goal difficult to attain. After all, our situations were quite different. I was a young, single mother with one young toddler. There were still hopes in my heart for a man I could build a home with, and many times I hungered for friends, companionship, and a secure future.

But baby Labron and I made it through life one day at a time. I loved this little boy God had given me, and I wanted to spend as much of my time with him as I possibly could. I wanted him to know that I was his mother. I had met too many parents whose children thought that their *sitters* were their mothers. I didn't want that for my son, so I made the sacrifices necessary to spend quality time with him. I traded in my luxury car for an economy car so that I wouldn't have to work overtime to make the payments. I took a job making less money and lowered my own standard of living in order to make sure that I was able to be with my child.

At nine o'clock one June night, after my shift at the store ended, I went straight to the sitter's house to pick up Labron. On the way home, Labron had fallen asleep, so I decided to make a quick stop at the car wash, hoping he would not wake up and be frightened while I was spraying down the car. I hurriedly dug through the bottom of my purse, trying to scrape up just enough change for the wash and rinse cycles.

I jumped out of the car, quickly inserted two quarters into the slot, and set the dial on the wash cycle. As I pulled back and forth on the soapy wand, I noticed that an unknown gentleman kept walking by. He seemed to be looking me up one side and down the other. I tried to ignore him. *"I'm single and happy that way,"* I thought. *"I'm really not interested in getting involved in another relationship or having my heart broken again . . . but this man sure is good looking!"*

I had to admit to myself that I was flattered that he found me attractive. I flashed him a little smile and went about my business. When the wash cycle finished, I walked around to set the dial to rinse and started to drop two more quarters in the slot. The first quarter dropped cleanly, but the second one fell from my grasping fingers and rolled into the drain. *Now* I was in a fix! I turned to see that Labron was still sleeping quietly. But it was dark outside, my car was covered in soap, and I was one quarter short of a rinse!

I couldn't leave Labron to go into the store for change, especially with this strange man walking by! The look of despair on my face must have been obvious, because this time around the man approached me and asked if I was having a problem. Embarrassed and desperate, I explained my situation and asked him to lend me a quarter. That opened the door of conversation for both of us.

Well, sometime during all this chaos, Labron woke up. Thankfully, he wasn't frightened. He was mesmerized by the water as it rinsed away the soap! As soon as I finished the job, I took Labron out of the car to go into the store for more change. I had to pay back the gentleman who had loaned me a quarter, didn't I? He may have been good looking, but I *certainly* didn't want to *owe* him anything. When I offered him his quarter back, he asked if he could hold Labron. I didn't want to seem rude after he had been kind enough to help me out of a tight spot, so I gave in. As soon as I had the baby back in my arms, I gave the stranger his quarter and fastened Labron into his car seat. I was ready to leave when the man introduced himself as Dan Robinson. I told him my name, and the conversation started up again. Two hours later, we parted—with *my* phone number in *his* pocket!

In Sickness and in Health

I praise the Lord every day for a car wash, a lost quarter, and for sending me the love of my life. Dan and I started dating one week later, and within two months we were married. When I met

Dan I was a twenty-one-year-old divorced mother. He was a twenty-eight year-old bachelor. I wasn't sure that he could handle a ready-made family, and I guess he could sense that doubt in me. He sat me down and told me that he loved both me and Labron with all of his heart. He said that we were all he wanted in life, so on Friday evening, August 27, 1982, Dan and I were married.

Since that blessed day when we became one (and not without a passel of trials), our love has grown sweeter every morning. Dan and I had both changed jobs just shortly before we married, so we couldn't take more time off work for a honeymoon. We had a quiet, intimate wedding with a small reception. That night we went home, and on Monday morning we went back to work.

The storm started just two weeks after we were married. I began mysteriously hemorrhaging, and the doctor's were unable to stop the bleeding. I had to undergo emergency surgery. I was out of work for three weeks, and since I had not fulfilled my ninety-day trial period, I lost my job. While I was recovering from surgery, Dan decided that once I recuperated I should stay at home with Labron rather than return to work. We knew that it would not be easy for us to live on just one income, but we made sacrifices and cut corners for me to be able to stay at home.

Five months after my surgery I knew that something was wrong. I had been struggling all along to get back to normal physically. My body just didn't seem right. Feeling like I had put Dan through so much already, I didn't want him to worry more, so I kept my fears to myself.

Although Dan never complained about the things we had no control over, I still couldn't help feeling guilty about them. He'd married into a ready-made family. Neither of us had major medical insurance when we married, so the bills from my surgery had quickly put us in debt. I tried not to add any additional stress to his life, but as time went on the fear that something was seriously wrong with me grew. My constant anxiety eventually drove me right into Dan's arms, where I poured out my fears to him. His response, as I should have known it would be, was loving concern.

First Comes Love, Then Comes Marriage . . .

Two days later, Dan and I walked into another storm at the doctor's office. Just five months into our marriage, we discovered that we were going to have a baby that we had not expected. I was eight weeks pregnant, and I had conceived while on birth control! Naturally, we were both speechless on the ride home.

I worried about Dan and how he was truly handling all of this. I knew marriage had been a big change in his life, and I was afraid I would lose him because of the adversities we were facing. Dan always seemed to sense my doubts and fears, and he reassured me that he was OK with everything that had happened in our marriage so far. He was always so supportive, and he told me that we would do whatever we had to do to make it.

Later that night we talked about the pregnancy. Although we both wanted another child, our plan had been to wait a few more years. God had a different plan—one that we were unable to see at the time. I often think now about how, even when we wanted no part of a life of righteousness, God was still working in our lives to fulfill His mighty plan.

The pregnancy was a difficult one. Two days after we found out that we were expecting, the doctor's office called me back in for more testing. They were concerned about some of the tests they had performed earlier. Tests results showed pre-cancerous cells on my cervix, but nothing could be done until after the baby was born. Dan and I both worried a great deal about the baby. Would he be born with cancer? Could I even carry him full term?

The doctors assured us that the baby would be fine, but that didn't take away the fear.

Still, the fear was the *least* of my problems during pregnancy. For nine months I battled infections, severe swelling, and premature labor. The infections kept my immune system totally drained and my body weak and fragile. I became an emotional basket case. My hormones were so off-balance that Dan could just look at me strangely and I would cry.

Meanwhile, my insecurities still wreaked havoc on our lives. I feared both disappointing and losing Dan. I worried about Labron and how he was handling all of this. He wasn't quite three years old yet and he had already had to adjust to a new daddy. Now he had a sibling on the way! My fears, insecurities, low self-esteem, and physical pain controlled me, affecting Dan and Labron. I seriously wondered if we could survive this.

Oh, Baby . . .

By the grace of God we did survive, and on September 21, 1983, our lives were blessed with a 7 lb., 12 oz. baby boy. We named him Kevin Dan Robinson. He was *beautiful*, but I noticed right away that there was something slightly wrong with him. There was something irregular about his bowels. There was blood in his stool and lots of it. He was having 25 to 30 bowel movements a day, and they were very acidic. His pediatrician sent us to Scottish Rite Children's Hospital in Atlanta, where we stayed for two weeks.

The doctors at Scottish Rite ran numerous tests on my new baby. It was so painful and stressful to watch as *time and time again* they placed needles in my two-week-old baby's head to draw blood for more tests. I would stand in the hallway and cry—praying for God to stop all of this. From the time they admitted my baby until they sent him home, I never left the hospital.

Though the doctors were unable to diagnose Kevin's problem, they were able to control it, and after two weeks they sent us home. Finally, when Kevin was two months old, they determined that an allergic reaction to milk and formula had irritated the lining of his intestines, causing acids to form and tiny blood veins to burst. Once his problem had been corrected, he began to grow like a weed.

I had been so caught up in seeing my baby well and at home with his family that my own health problems had ceased to worry me. Now that Kevin was OK, I had to face my pre-cancerous cells again. I went back to the doctor for a check-up, for further testing, and to decide what our best treatment approach for this problem should be. For the time, the doctors felt that cauterization would be the most appropriate treatment. I went through the prescribed procedure, and it seemed to be effective.

Once the pre-cancerous cells had been treated, life settled down for our family. All four of us—happy and healthy—were finally at home together. Labron had adjusted well to the recent changes in the family, and we looked forward to some type of normality in our lives. Just being at home together seemed to bring a peace that none of us had known for months. I settled both of the boys into a normal daily routine and tried to make life as easy as possible for Dan.

Unholy Deadlock

When the medical bills started coming in for both Kevin and me, Dan was forced to work as much overtime as possible. I thought about going back to work just to help relieve this financial strain, but Dan felt like the kids really needed me to be at home with them. I didn't argue with him because I hated the thought of leaving my children with strangers. For the next year, I stayed at home with the boys, and it seemed as if our family was on an uphill climb. With only one income, we had managed to survive and we were doing the best we could with our medical bills.

Except for a few minor health problems, things were going well. However, the stress and strain that Dan and I had faced during the first two years of our marriage had taken their toll on our relationship, and our marriage became very distant. I worried constantly about the bills. I lived with fear daily that, because of everything we had been through, I would lose Dan. We were doing everything we could to pay all of the doctors and hospitals, but it just wasn't enough.

Creditors and collection agencies were calling every day. In frustration, I would slam the phone down and weep uncontrollably. Dan would come in exhausted from a long day at work and collapse in a deep sleep on the couch. Naturally (because I'm from Venus and he's from Mars), I thought that he just didn't care about our problems, especially mine. We no longer communicated as we once had. Every conversation ended up as an argument, with both of us saying things we did not mean. Each night we went to bed either exhausted or angry. There was no time or energy for making things right with one another, either.

Just as the stress between us was reaching a breaking point, Dan took a new job and our less-stressed relationship was able to mend. We made other changes, too. In order to be closer to Dan's work, we moved back to my hometown. We knew we needed some drastic change in our lives, and the move somehow gave both of us hope for a brighter future. For one thing, our rent decreased by over $100 a month. We applied the extra money to our medical bills. The changes took much of the stress off of our lives, and Dan and I drew closer once again. Although neither of us was living for the Lord at that time, His loving hand was *even then* at work in our lives.

By January of 1985 we were completely moved and settled in our new home. The kids loved the change, and so did I. We moved from a small, two-bedroom trailer into a three-bedroom house. Kevin was sixteen months old, and Labron was already four-and-a-half, so they appreciated having rooms of their own. I was excited to be back in my hometown . . . just a few miles from my parents and all of my sisters. We had been raised as a very close family, with unconditional love and a desire to bear one another's burdens. Just being near them again gave me a sense of security and stability in my life.

Sickness Strikes Again

One Saturday evening that January, I invited Debra and her husband over for dinner. As couples, we'd had the best time playing with the kids and playing cards after the children went to bed. Although it was late when Debra and Lemuel left, I didn't want to leave the mess until morning. The kids had left toys and playthings lying on the hardwood floors throughout the house, so I walked room to room picking up and cleaning.

I walked into the living room and promptly stepped on a Tonka truck. On those hardwood floors, the truck rolled right out from under me—taking my feet with it. Then I hit the floor back-of-my-head first, and was instantly, although temporarily, paralyzed. Dan called an ambulance, and they rushed me to the hospital. The emergency room doctors didn't know what to do for me, so they gave me some medicine and sent me home. When we got home later, though the paralysis had faded, I was still unable to use my limbs to full capacity.

For a full week after my fall I lay in the bed with pain, numbness, and muscle spasms. My head hurt profusely. Primarily, I had a deep, constant pain in the back of my head that would *not* go away. I experienced blurred vision and nausea. Because I was unable to take care of the children, Dan had already missed two days of work.

As the days passed, my agony increased. I just could not live with the headache any longer. I went to my sister's house and asked her to take me to the hospital. "If I don't get help for this pain in my head, Dolly, I'm going to die," I told her.

Besides the head pain, my arms still were not working fully, and my legs were as limber as wet dishrags. "Something is very wrong," I thought. My body was *not* functioning properly.

I was admitted to Cobb General Hospital in Austell, Georgia, where I was examined and tested by a staff of neurologists. The fall

I had taken a week earlier had bruised my brain and pinched both a nerve in my neck and one in my back. The doctors also found scar tissue on another part of my brain (caused by an accident I'd had as a child.) For two weeks, I stayed in the hospital for extensive testing and physical therapy three times a day. During this testing, the doctors also found more pre-cancerous cells.

The pre-cancerous cells posed a threat, but the doctors wanted to give my body time to heal from the therapy and treatments before treating me for anything else. I was released from the hospital in January, and they scheduled me for a partial hysterectomy in February.

Since the cells had come back after the cauterization, the doctors felt that surgery would be the most effective remedy. Thankfully, Dan's major medical insurance coverage had kicked in, so the medical bills did not add quite so much strain to our lives this time.

The surgery was a complete success. The doctors were able to remove *all* of my pre-cancerous cells, and I did not require any further treatment after surgery. To my amazement, even my back pain subsided once the hysterectomy had been done. I returned home feeling better than I had felt in years. After eight weeks, the doctor released me from his care and I was doing great.

Calm Before the Storm

In May of 1985, Dan and I decided to take the honeymoon we had never had. After so many physical trials, we definitely needed a break, so we took advantage of the fact that I was now feeling so well. We headed to Gatlinburg, Tennessee, with a couple who were close friends of ours, for a weekend getaway. My sister Carolyn had volunteered to take care of our children for the weekend, so I knew they would be in good hands. We couldn't wait to get away and have a little fun together.

We arrived in Gatlinburg late Friday evening and rented a nice motel room with a balcony over the river. It was one of those rare, special evenings in a relationship that seem to make the hard times almost worthwhile. And we had *such* a great time together.

Standing on the balcony of our room overlooking the river, Dan and I fell in love all over again. We laughed, we cried, and we shared our true feelings with one another. The peacefulness of that shared moment, with the soothing sounds of the river and the mutual pledge of a better future, gave us hope that we could start over again, fresh and new, when we got home. With all of my physical problems taken care of, we could return with the happy anticipation of *no more illnesses* or hospitals.

After three years of marriage, Dan and I had learned that it's important to make time for romance and for just enjoying one another—as well as friends. We had come with Dan's best friend Lyndon and his wife, Sharon, and, in a rare return to the carefree days of our youth, the four of us thoroughly enjoyed each other. We raced go-karts and rode the chair lifts; we *shopped until we dropped.* We had set out to enjoy the weekend, and we did!

We had promised Debra that we'd be back in time to have dinner at her house at around 5:00 P.M. Sunday evening, so we left for home early Sunday morning. Looking back on the long, lovely drive home, I could not have had more hope for our future than I did at that moment. Our love was renewed, and my health was restored. *"We have so much to live for and so much to look forward to,"* I thought, dozing off now and then along the way.

I was eager to see the children. I had missed them both so much, but it had done us all good to take a short break from one another. However, the effects of our weekend of fun and the long ride home were clearly setting in by the time we arrived at Debra's.

I had picked up a slight but nagging headache somewhere along the journey. The pain lingered, and by the time we arrived for dinner my headache had grown much worse. I attributed the pain to fatigue from the trip. *"Once I've rested I'll be fine,"* I thought. As we sat down to dinner, I remember thinking that the pain was overwhelming. And that's the last thing I remembered!

Now, two weeks later, here I am . . . waking up in Debra's living room recliner, surrounded by loving and concerned family members. "What's going on, Debra?" I asked. "Did we have dinner? Where are the children?"

"Never mind about that now, Brenda. You've been in and out of doctor's offices and hospitals for two weeks," said my sister. "For awhile there, we were afraid we were going to lose you completely," she replied.

My diagnosis? *Grand mal* epileptic seizures.

Chapter 3
Seizure!

n July of 1987, I began to succumb to feelings of hope-lessness. I had been having seizures for two years, and they weren't showing any signs of getting better. Dan's insurance had dropped me for being high risk, so once again we were without major medical insurance. *"I'm not sure how much more either of us can handle,"* I thought, with a heavy sigh of hopelessness and despair.

For the past two years I had been a medical guinea pig, with physicians trying every new treatment and test under the sun on me to discover the nature of the problem and determine a possible cure. The doctors finally determined that a section of bruise and scar tissue on my brain had not healed completely. This, they said, was the reason for my seizures.

Every new medicine that needed to be tested for seizure patients was tested on me, but none had worked. At one point we were spending nearly $400 per month at the pharmacy alone, and none of these medicines were doing me any good. In addition, my medical bills had soared to over $100,000. Creditors were calling everyday.

At this time, I was having seizures an average of nine to twelve times monthly. Each time one occurred, it would leave me paralyzed on the right side, unable to speak, and without my memory for several days. I would become a virtual invalid, having to be fed and bathed by someone else. I couldn't be left alone for fear that I would seize and hurt myself. At times I had broken bones or carpet-burned my face during hard convulsive seizures, and no one wanted to take the chance of more serious injuries by leaving me alone. Feeling like a burden and unable to properly care for my husband and children, I began to wonder seriously if there was any reason to continue living at all.

Heavy Burdens

Dan—my Rock of Gibralter—was beginning to grow weary, too. Though he never complained, the lines in his face and the gray in his hair signified his increasing stress and fatigue. Once a man asked Dan how many seizures I had had. Dan told him that if he'd count the number of gray hairs on his head, he'd know. I choked back tears, realizing that Dan truly never had a gray hair until after I had had my first seizure.

I can understand why he turned gray so fast. He would work all day, then have to come home and take care of me and the boys all evening. I thank God often that Dan never left me for someone else or for a better life. Despite our grueling circumstances, he was faithful.

My seizures usually started around eight or nine o'clock at night, and they would continue until two or three in the morning. Often it wasn't just *one* seizure. There were many times when I would have four or five attacks in eight hours. The convulsions usually intensified my back condition, causing me to go into muscle spasms. That would keep me up for the rest of the night fighting headaches and back pain.

There were countless nights when Dan had to call one of my sisters or my mother to come help him work with me after a seizure, and they faithfully came every time. In the throes of a seizure, my muscles would contract tightly, causing my body to draw up. Sometimes they had to work on my muscles all night just to get me to where I could relax. Without the willing sacrifices of my family members, I don't know how we would have made it.

Dan never slept through one peaceful night in the six years I was sick with epilepsy. If I just moved my arm, he would grab frantically for me, thinking that I was having a seizure. The doctors had told Dan that one blow to my head could kill me, so he had to try to keep me from hitting my head at all costs. They also told him that my seizures were so hard that the strain on my body would take my life within five years. The doctors fully expected me to have a massive heart attack and die while seizing. Dan was afraid that each seizure would be my last. During this dark time, we really did not have much hope at all for a recovery.

Once Dan's insurance dropped me, getting proper medical attention became almost impossible. Because we didn't have any insurance, it seemed as though we were pushed to the side and neglected by the medical community . . . *another degrading and painful experience.*

One night I had several seizures and was unconscious for quite some time. Dan called an ambulance to take me to the emergency room. The doctors and nurses had never seen seizures as violent as mine. They didn't know what to do. One of the nurses shoved a tongue depressor in my mouth, strapped me to a stretcher, and left me alone with Dan. Sadly, we'd seen sides of the medical industry that most people never have, and this didn't make us want to go back for more!

Dan learned to keep me at home and tend to me the best he could. He always made sure that my prescriptions were filled—even if he had to let one of our bills go unpaid to do it. For the most part, I leaned on his strength to endure my illness. The depth of his patience and faithfulness overwhelmed me at times. Incredibly, Dan never let the seizures come between us or push him away. Instead, we drew closer and grew stronger. Through the course of this illness, marriage and *life itself* took on a whole new, precious meaning for both of us. And amazingly, though we as yet had no idea just how closely and powerfully, God was still working in our lives.

"Who are those kids?"

The hardest aspect of the seizures for me was the memory loss. There were times when I wouldn't even know Dan or my children. I remember one particular night when I'd had several seizures, and my memory was gone. I couldn't walk or talk, and Dan had put me on the couch so he could keep an eye on me. I saw two boys playing on the floor, but I had no idea who they were. In my mind I said, *"Lord, who are those kids playing in the floor?"* Just then Kevin, who was only four years old at the time, immediately walked over to where I was. He pulled himself up on my lap and, just like he knew what I was thinking, said, "Mama, I love you, and God is going to fix you someday, and you are going to be well." Even though I still wasn't living for Him, God was speaking to me and loving me through my own children.

It seemed like the worst times for Dan were the instances in which the seizures paralyzed my speech. When this happened, he often became frustrated by his inability to understand what I was trying to say to him. Usually, my right arm would be paralyzed and the muscles in my left arm would be drawn, making it unusable as well. I couldn't speak or write, so I tried to use body language, but it didn't always work!

One night in particular stands out in my mind. Dan was still hand-feeding me, and we hadn't been through eating dinner long when I was ready for something to drink. I tried unsuccessfully to make Dan understand what I wanted, but he just walked away in frustration. Labron, now six years old, said, "Daddy, Mama wants something to drink. It's been about thirty minutes since she had dinner, and she always drinks a Coke about thirty minutes after she eats."

I was amazed that Labron had been watching me so closely that he knew my habitual dining patterns exactly! My heart swelled with love for my precious little boy.

Still, I couldn't stand being such a burden to my family. *"This isn't what a wife and mother is supposed to be doing—being waited on hand and foot,"* I thought. I lost the will to live. I begged Dan and the rest of my family to put me away in a home somewhere so my children wouldn't have to watch me live in this horrible condition. I wanted Dan to move on with his life, too, because he deserved better. Slowly but surely, I sank into a deep depression.

My mind rehearsed, over and over, the hopeless, endlessly frustrating facts. I had been stripped of everything that most people take for granted. At twenty-six years of age, I lost the legal right to drive a vehicle. Dan had put ceiling fans in every room of the new home we had built, and we couldn't even use them because the rotation triggered my seizures. Family portraits were out of the question because the flash would trigger a seizure, too. I was robbed even of my privacy, since even when I took a bath someone had to be with me. My seizures were so unpredictable that the family feared I'd have one in the bathtub and drown. Finally, feeling isolated and angry, my mental state disintegrated into a full-blown self-pity that I couldn't shake for weeks.

Thanks for the Memories

I had forgotten that my children needed their mother. I had forgotten about Dan's need for a wife. I had forgotten that my mother needed her daughter. I could think of no one's feelings but my own. I decided I would be doing everyone else a favor by releasing them from the burden of caring for me, and to accomplish just that I had planned my own death.

"Exit Plan"

I didn't have any trouble justifying suicide. The seizures obviously weren't going to get any better, and I couldn't even raise my own children in the kind of shape I was in. Dan would surely be better off alone or with someone who could be a true wife to him. My mother had just lost my older brother, Dee, who also suffered from seizures, then died with a brain tumor at the age of twenty-seven. It didn't seem fair for her to have to endure seeing a child suffer from seizures—and possibly death—all over again. I couldn't see a better solution to any of these problems, so quietly, carefully, I formulated my "exit plan." But God had something else in mind. He intervened right on time.

No one knew that I had planned to take my life, especially not my mother, but she showed up at my house with my sister, Dolly, on the day I was going to commit suicide. The two of them sat me down, and with *tough love* they talked me right out of my plan to end my life. Somehow, they seemed to know exactly how I felt about life. "Still, you can't continue to be so selfish," Dolly said, as I hung my head in sorrow. "You have to learn to accept your illness, get up out of your self-pity, and go on." Her frank words pierced through my cloud of darkness, but my pride and anger fought them at first.

Mother looked me right in the eyes and said, "God has a great plan for your life, Brenda, and He can use this for His glory if you'll let Him." She may have been right, but it didn't bring me much comfort at the moment. *They just don't seem to understand, do they?* I thought.

"I'm going to die," I responded. "It's only a matter of time; even the doctors have told me so. Don't you get it?" I cried. "You're going to lose me soon anyway, so why should I hang on any longer?" I reasoned.

Dolly had had enough of my wallowing in self-pity. "I wish you'd go on and die and get out of my way! I'll take your kids and raise them right because they sure don't have a fit mother now if you've given up on life," she replied.

I was furious with her. How could she *dare* talk to me that way? I was the one dying here! Mother continued trying to encourage me. She pointed out all of the positives about my condition and told me to stop dwelling on the negatives. Once again, the gentle influence of my godly mother and a sister with the *courage to confront* had made a miraculous difference in my life

Seize the Day!

Once Mother and Dolly were gone, I realized that all thoughts of suicide had left my mind. Nothing in my circumstances had actually changed, but from *that* day on I was determined to live. I knew I had to go on, and that it would be an uphill climb. We were about to lose everything we had due to overwhelming financial debts, and I was still very ill.

Being husband, provider, and father had caused Dan to grow more and more defeated, hopeless, and mentally drained. Our bills were behind, our credit ruined. In order to be close to home and work his own hours in case something happened to me, Dan had been forced to go into business for himself. Business was slow and groceries were hard to come by, but we had too much pride to ask for help. I could see Dan folding under the pressure, and he had every right to do so. I knew that it was time for me to be *his* strength for a while.

Determined to take the *lemons* in my life and make lemonade out of them, my resolve to live was growing stronger day by day. I learned to savor every moment I had with my children. I made up my mind to "seize instead of being seized." My condition had controlled me long enough! It was time to *deal* with it instead of dwelling on it.

To do this, I knew I would have to look at my seizures in a whole new light. To deal with them from a position of strength, I could no longer afford to view myself as the victim. I had to see my *family* members as the true victims of my illness. I knew how I had felt for the last two years, but now I needed to know *their* side of the story. I had so many questions for my whole family, questions that I had been afraid to ask for two years.

I wanted to know why Dan had stayed with me through the years. Why had Debra and Dolly been so faithful to us when we had been forsaken by so many others? How was Mother able to stay so strong, even after losing a son? As I made the rounds to family members, everyone was so gracious to answer my questions and to try and help me deal with my situation.

The more I learned from my family, the greater I realized that *they* truly were the victims in this situation. Like Job himself, their unconditional love for me had been tested and tried, yet they'd come through it with pure hearts—shining brighter than gold.

Greater Love Hath No Man

Every day I lived in tortuous fear of losing Dan, yet he always remained faithful to me. I knew it had to be hard on him. I questioned him about what kept him by my side. At the time, he had no answer. Today we know that it was God who kept him there.

Dan admits that there were times when leaving crossed his mind. Looking back at everything we went through, Dan recalls, "A lot of mornings I just wanted to get in my car and leave. A lot of times, when the medical bills would come, I wanted to throw away the bills and just run away. In my mind, I wanted to be somewhere else, but in my heart I knew I couldn't leave because *Jesus* had a hold on me."

I remember having an excruciating headache one night after I had been through several seizures. When I regained consciousness, Dan had me cradled in his arms in a fetal position, and he was crying out loud and praying to God, "Lord, if she has any pain, let me carry it for her so she can rest." I don't know if Dan actually took my headache, but it was gone instantly. I knew at this moment that his love for me was something greater than an ordinary love.

I'm so glad that God was working in our lives long before we were working in His kingdom. Because I know this to be true, I am able to assure others that He is at work in their lives, too. In your dysfunctional childhood, in your marital strife, in sickness and in health, God is at work in your life—carrying you along to an ever-increasing awareness of His love and grace.

Dan didn't know what kept him by my side; he just knew he couldn't leave me. There were many times when I couldn't be the wife to Dan that a man needs, and I'm sure that, had God not had His hand on our lives, the financial stress alone could have driven him away.

It didn't matter to me that Dan couldn't explain the reason that he stayed by my side. Just knowing that he was there helped give me the desire to keep going. Still, I wanted to know how my seizures had been affecting him.

Watching me have the seizures was hard on him, Dan said, but the two things that he found hardest to deal with were the aftermath of my seizures and my constant feelings of inadequacy. Each time I had a series of seizures, I would come out of them disoriented and confused. My memory would be gone, and I was often paralyzed and unable to speak. When the seizures were really bad, I couldn't even remember Dan or my boys after resurfacing. Frightened by the "strangers" around me, I would refuse to let them help me. Unable to talk, I couldn't ask for someone familiar, and Dan was left feeling helpless and hopeless.

My feelings of inadequacy kept both of us feeling inadequate. I was insecure as a woman, a wife, and a mother. I knew that no man wanted a wife who stayed paralyzed and disfigured most of the time, so I went overboard trying to compensate for my shortcomings. What I could do I wanted to do perfectly, and I was driving everyone crazy in the process. I was so afraid of losing Dan that I became jealous and overbearing. So, when my seizures weren't controlling our lives, my emotions were.

Life was truly difficult for Dan under those circumstances, but he remained faithful for reasons he couldn't explain. I wondered if Debra, Dolly, and Mother had also been victimized by my seizures. For my own sake, I had to know.

Debra usually stayed with me during the day, and I couldn't have made it without her. She took care of me and my family all day—then went home and took care of her own family every evening. She cleaned house, washed clothes, and cooked dinner for us all the time. Without ever having to be asked, she just did what had to be done. Once I had been healed, I couldn't find the words to tell Debra how much I appreciated her dedication and many sacrifices for me and for our family, so I tried to put them in this little poem:

Sister and Friend

I have never forgotten the words you would say.
or the special encouragement you gave every day.
"It'll be all right," you said, with words so kind.
It always seemed that you could read my mind.
You always prayed, "God, touch her if you will."
And now, from sickness I've been healed.
If I could give you a crown for all that you have done,
I would make real sure that you got the prettiest one.
You're my sister—a very special sister, you see,
A blessing from God, given personally to me.
Yet more than just a sister; Oh, yes, much more indeed . . .
You're the friend that's always been there in my greatest time of need.
I've never been able to tell you exactly how I feel.
So I pray that through this poem my feelings will be revealed.
And I thank you, Debra Evans, for all the love you share,
For all the times you've helped me, and the burdens you gladly bear.
For the role of "Lady Proverbs," if someone I had to choose,
I know without a doubt your feet would fill her shoes.

Debra seemed to be a tower of strength, but below the surface *she also* felt pain and hopelessness. When I went to her with my nagging questions, the word she used to describe the seizures was "terrorizing." So Debra, too, was terrorized by helplessness and fear. If I went into a seizure, the only thing she could do was try to prevent me from hurting myself—and the seizures were so hard that even something that simple was almost impossible for one person.

I could always count on Debra to help me out in any way she was able. It's just her nature to do things for others. She has a true servant's heart. But the seizures left her feeling helpless because there just wasn't anything she could do to help.

Debra's feelings of helplessness were made worse by her own fears. With our brother Dee's death so fresh on everyone's minds, she was desperately afraid of losing *me* also. Although she hoped I would get better some day, she still lived with the fear that I would die. My seizures were so different from Dee's that she didn't fear a brain tumor. Debra's fear was that I would seize while driving or that a seizure would be so hard that it would cause me to have a massive heart attack.

In our frank, private talk, Debra admitted to me that she, too, grew tired of the seizures, but that our strong family bond had kept her by my side. It was that same family bond that kept my sister Dolly from walking away from it all, as well.

"Precious Little Burden"

Dolly has always been a strong, level-headed person, and just having her around gave me a sense of security. She was usually the one Dan called on for help in the middle of the night when the seizures and their aftermath became more than he could handle alone. Dolly had to be with me so often that she soon was able to tell when I was going to have a seizure just by my appearance.

A strong woman who I've always deeply admired, her strength was amazing. The hardest part of it all for her was when I gave up the will to live. She says of the seizures now, "It was hard, but I handled it. I guess I always knew that the Lord was going to heal you one day."

Dolly just seemed to accept my seizures as part of life; they didn't seem to affect her much at all. She once said, "The Lord gave me so much strength that it didn't even upset me when you would have seizures, but it broke my heart." It broke her heart because I was so debilitated after the seizures. She didn't like to see me frightened and disoriented. My inability to recognize my own husband and children just tore her heart out. She admits now that there were times when it all became too much for her, and that when she was alone she would break down emotionally from the stress of it all.

My sister Dolly's love was a tough love. She wouldn't let me be defeated by my seizures or the effect that they had on me. After a seizure, I'd often let my emotions get out of control due to the frustration of being unable to communicate my needs to the person trying to help me. People who didn't know Dolly often thought that she treated me cruelly in times like that. Often as she was feeding me I'd get angry because she wasn't feeding me fast enough. Unable to vent my frustrations in any other way, I would cry. Jokingly, Dolly would say, "If you don't hush, I'm gonna smack you." I knew it had to be frustrating for her, too. I would laugh, but others thought she was just being mean to me. I recognized it, though, as her own particular brand of *tough love.*

And it was probably Dolly's tough love that saved my life when I had given up the will to live. Still, I stayed furious with her for months for the things she'd said. During that time, she'd call just to see if I had died yet, and I'd hang up on her. She refused to feel sorry for me—or to let me feel sorry for myself. It hurt, but later I had to thank her for it. Although it made me mad, I had to admit to myself that she was right. Her tough love made me realize just how ugly my self-pity had become.

One of the most memorable things about the seizures for Dolly, she reported, happened on a night when we all thought that I was going to die. I had been through a series of seizures, and I had been in tremors nonstop for an hour and fifteen minutes. Usually, the tremors only lasted for a few minutes. Our pastor was there that night, too.

Though I couldn't communicate with anyone around me, inside I was pleading with the Lord. *"Either deliver me from the pain, Lord, or take me now,"* I prayed. I could literally feel my organs collapsing from the convulsions. My pastor and his wife gathered around me with Dan and Dolly, and they began to pray. Instantly, the tremors stopped. "It was unbelievable," Dolly says now, "I really thought that the Lord had come back. It was awesome."

This type of seizure would usually leave me unable to speak, but this time I came out of it telling them all what I had seen. I was in the midst of heavenly activity. Angels had been camped about me, and I perceived that *Jesus* Himself had been walking all around me. My family and friends hadn't seen the vision, as I had, but they *had* all felt the presence of the Lord in the room that night. When I looked over at Dolly, she was as white as a sheet and speechless. I knew that she had sensed God's presence—just by the look on her face.

To Dolly, I was her "Precious Little Burden." She gave me that nickname because of everything we went through while I was having seizures. There were many nights when Dan would call her, and she'd jump out of the bed barefooted and in her pajamas to come help him out. Sometimes she'd work on the muscle spasms I was having for hours. At other times I refused to be comforted unless I could get out of the house. There were many nights when she and Dan would have to take me out to the park and just let me walk the track at two or three o'clock in the morning.

There were also times when my medications caused hallucinations, and I would insist that someone kill the bugs that only I could see. It's a wonder that everyone didn't call me *some kind of burden*. In December of 1992, after I had been healed, I wrote this little poem for Dolly.

My "Precious Little Blessing"

My "Precious Little Burden"
is what you always said—
A personal little joke
to let me know you cared.
In hard times you would say it,
God knows, we've shared a few.
I never would have made it
Had it not been for you.
You pushed me one step further,
You never left my side.
You were always there to comfort me,
The many times I cried.
Together we rejoice now,
For God saw fit to heal
your "Precious Little Burden,"
who once was very ill.
I really appreciate you, Dolly,
For all the things you did,

The many nights you sacrificed,
and the nights spent by my bed.
You're "My Precious Little Blessing,"
and those are words I say
to my Heavenly Father each morning
when I kneel down to pray.

Of course, Dolly wasn't my only "Precious Little Blessing." God knows I couldn't have made it without Debra and Dan, and I'll never forget how well the children handled it all. Sometimes I think it didn't leave a lasting impression on their lives. They were so young that it probably seemed par for the course to them, but I couldn't have made it without them. Once, when Kevin was only four-years-old, I was cooking dinner and felt myself slipping into a seizure. The towel I was holding caught fire, and Kevin calmly took it from me and put it out. When he was in the ninth grade, he was assigned to write an essay in English class. This is what he wrote:

My Greatest Gift

My life has been rough, but my mom's has been worse. She had serious seizures for six years. She had what you call *grand mal* epileptic seizures. Almost anything could trigger her seizures. When riding in a car, oncoming cars passing would make her have a seizure. Flashing lights or sun shining through the trees could cause her to have seizures. There wasn't a day that went by that Mom did not have at least one seizure. Sometimes she would have several seizures a day.

Every time Mom had a seizure it would paralyze her vocal chords, and she could not talk. She would be paralyzed on the right side of her body and crippled. She had a very rough life. She could not work or do anything, but at least she still had her faith in God.

We went to church all the time and had a singing group. When Mom started singing, God made it where the seizures would not take her voice away, but she would still be crippled. Usually my dad would hold her up as she sang. Although we travel throughout the United States singing now, at the time the seizures kept us close to home.

The next problem we faced was doctor's bills. Mom had to go to the hospital or the doctor's office all the time, and that made it tough on us to pay our bills. In just eight years we had built up over $80,000 in hospital and doctor bills. We had also just built a brand new house that we had to pay for, but God pulled us through. However, Mom still had her seizures every day, and when Mom wasn't down because of her seizures we were traveling most every weekend to sing.

When she was down from a seizure Mom would lie on the bed and read her Bible for six to eight hours a day. She read and studied the Bible every day. She ended up reading the Bible through twelve times and still reads and studies to this day. She established a women's ministry and put a newsletter out every month. She and some of her friends wrote in the newsletter. My mom also became a songwriter and author. She wrote many songs and books. Still, Mom was very sick.

One day mom had to go to the doctor, and he found some things wrong with her bladder. She had to have bladder surgery, and she was in the bed for weeks. Mom recovered very slowly from this surgery because every time she got a little better the seizures would set her back again, but she still kept her faith in God's power to answer prayer.

Mom prayed three times a day: at 9:00 A.M., she would pray for her family; at 12:00 P.M., she would pray for others; and at 9:00 P.M., she would pray for anything. Each time she prayed she would ask God to heal her.

I guess my seizures *did* have a lasting impression on the kids, but the boys seemed to handle my illness better than most adults. They truly were *my precious little blessings.* My mother was another special blessing during those six years. She was sick and frail, so there was little she could do to help me *physically* during a seizure. But she was often my strength and comfort afterwards. Like Debra, she was a tower of strength for my sake. Mom never let me believe that I wouldn't be healed someday.

Despite her faith, the seizures were stressful on my mother. She believed that God had the power to heal me, yet each time I seized she feared this would be the one to take me. Still, she never let her faith waver in my presence. It wasn't until several years later that I learned of her well-hidden fears.

It was only my mother's personal and intimate relationship with God that gave her peace about my seizures. When I called her for encouragement, she always tried to share that peace with me. She reminded me constantly that someday I would be healed, if not in this lifetime then when I got home with Jesus. As comforting as her words were, I longed to know this peace for myself. And I knew that the only place I could find the kind of peace my mother had would be within the kind of love affair that she had with Jesus.

Chapter 4

The Love Affair

As the third year of seizures began, I was having five to ten seizures a day. Just when I would begin to recover from one series of seizures, with my ability to speak and my memory restored, I'd go headlong into another. If I wasn't having seizures, I was struggling to recover from them. It seemed as though I was never completely well—even for one full day.

My fight to survive was not easy, but I knew now that I had to be strong for my family's sake. For two years they'd refused to break on me, and I didn't want to let them down. Still, it was hard not to give up, especially on days when Murphy's Law ("Anything that *can* go wrong, *will*") seemed to be ruling.

I'm sure you're familiar with the kind of days I'm referring to here—the kind when frustrations just *don't* seem to end. The bills are running late, there aren't enough hours in the day to accomplish what needs to be done, everyone needs your undivided attention at the same time, your head hurts, there's nothing in the cabinet to fix for dinner, the phone rings off the hook, you run late all day, and you fight with your spouse all night! Maybe I'm the only one who ever has days like these, but I'm sure you understand how they make it easy to want to give up.

Throughout my six years of seizures we had many days like that. To be honest, we still do—but at that time in our lives that kind of day seemed especially hopeless and unbearable. It was hard to come up with enough money every month to buy my needed medications. I often pleaded with Dan to use the money to pay the bills instead, but he always refused my wishes. I felt like our bills were more important than my health, but Dan insisted that I have the medicine before anything else was paid. Sadly, our strained finances caused many arguments in those days.

When Dan and I weren't arguing about finances, we were arguing about marital issues. We argued about which bills should be paid and which ones could wait another week or two. We argued about the way I took care of myself and how closely I followed doctor's orders. Dan's sincere care caused him to be protective of me, but I found him *overprotective*. I'm not sure which one of us had the highest stress level, but I'm sure it was a close race!

Of course, money was tighter than ever, which only added to our stress and tension. Dan's business was still trying to get off the ground, and work was hard to come by. As is most often the case, we both chose to blame the other for our hard times. I thought Dan should be working more, and he thought that he wouldn't have to kill himself in order to make us a living if I would take better care of myself. In all honesty, we were both giving life our very best. However, misery loves company, so Dan and I became *misery buddies.*

Misery

The communication gap that formed between Dan and me in the third year of my epilepsy almost destroyed our marriage. At one point, we were only days away from a divorce. In fact, I had determined to leave Dan, and he was determined to let me go. Through the weight of heavy circumstance, we had grown tired and defeated, and both of us felt like the negatives finally outweighed the positives in our relationship.

The medical bills had pushed us over the edge financially. My stubbornness and independence drove Dan further and further away. His pride and his need to be in control often prevented us from receiving the outside help we needed, and that was hard on the whole family. I remember one night when the four of us sat down to eat dinner. All we had was one pack of crackers, a can of pork and beans, and four slices of bread. It wasn't just Dan's pride that hurt us; I didn't want anyone to know that we were in that kind of shape, either. So, *two* prideful people hid their need from friends and family. God surely had His work cut out for Him!

Even though we were both very ready to give up on our marriage, we never separated. Dan was waiting for me to leave, but I wanted *him* to go. I had decided that it would be much easier for him to find somewhere else to go than it would be for me. If I left, I would have to take the boys with me. He could go alone. Our stubbornness kept us together, but it didn't bridge the divide between us. We had become distant and passive in our relationship. We were both miserable inside.

Even though our relationship was struggling, Dan was still right there with me when I needed him most. The seizures were still coming on like clockwork, and Dan always took care of me when they came. I couldn't understand why. I wanted him gone, and he wanted to go, but if I got sick he stayed right by my side without complaining until I got well. I just couldn't figure out *what* was wrong with our relationship.

One day, after a series of seizures, I asked Dan why he stayed with me. I accused him of hating me, and I told him that I couldn't understand why he kept hanging around where he really didn't want to be. With tears in his eyes he faithfully answered my questions. As sincerely as he could he said, "Brenda, you have me all wrong. I don't hate you. I hate our circumstances. I stay with you because I love you, and I care about us and our children."

He continued, "My love for you is greater than any of our circumstances. I really don't want to leave you, and I certainly don't want a divorce." I felt like dirt. I had treated him so badly for the past few months simply because we had failed to communicate and share our true feelings with one another. From that point on, I was determined to communicate about everything in order to change our marriage. I never wanted to take the chance of losing him again over a failure to talk out our problems.

Communication was not our only problem. I remember the day I came to the realization that if our circumstances didn't change soon, we would both die. I would die from the seizures, and Dan would die from stress. Looking at my strained, graying husband, I could literally see it coming. We had both gotten as far down as we could go. We were in a state of total brokenness.

People told us everyday that we would never amount to anything because we owed over $100,000 in medical bills. Sometimes it seemed like others *thrived* on running us down. I felt so out of control in my whole life. At twenty-six years of age, I was considered an invalid. The doctors had given me *no hope* of ever being any better. As a matter of fact, they expected me to get worse!

Another heartache was that many of my dearest and best friends had abandoned me when I started having seizures. My uncontrollable seizing made them feel uncomfortable, and they didn't want any part of it. I felt I had become a burden to my sisters, was a poor excuse for a mother, and an even worse wife. Dan felt like a failure as a husband and a provider. It didn't matter how much money he brought home, it was never enough to meet the financial demands in our lives.

Dan also felt abandoned by friends. His pride was broken, and his motivation to survive had nearly left him. By this time, my husband viewed life as unfair; he struggled with the notion we had been given a pretty raw deal from God as a couple and a family.

Everyone had a comment or some advice, but no one had any real *solutions*. Many professing Christians told us that we should file bankruptcy, but Dan always rejected that idea. We both had been raised to pay our bills. Bankruptcy was *not* an option. Despite the heavy financial pressures, we praise God for His protection and provision at that time. To this day, we have never filed any type of bankruptcy. We just struggled along . . . doing the best we could.

Convicted!

One day in the early summer of 1986, my brokenness brought me to my knees. There was such a void in my life. We had searched near and far, but no one *anywhere* could offer us any hope for our lives. Each breath I took felt like a knife being stabbed into my chest. I knew that it was stress, one of the leading killers in America, and now it was coming after Dan and me!

Why, Lord, Why?

Sometimes life just doesn't present us with any easy choices. I didn't want to live in my circumstances any longer, but I didn't want to die, either. I wanted to live long enough to see my children grown and able to take care of themselves. In my despair, still full of anger and bitterness, I cried out to God. I asked God why He'd let this happen to me.

At the top of my lungs I screamed out to God that He was supposed to be a God of love. He was supposed to love people, not hurt them and let these kinds of things happen to them. I released all the years of my anger, rebellion, hurt, and rejection on God. I questioned His motives and intentions—and my entire relationship with Him. I questioned His love for me. But like Dan and everyone else I had questioned before, God, too, was faithful to answer me.

The first thing I had to know was where I truly stood with God. Truthfully, I had doubted my salvation since the age of sixteen. Though I had been raised to believe in eternal security, I just couldn't comprehend God being able to love me after all that I had done through the years. Maybe I had never been born again. Would

God really allow one of His children to wander out into the world, as I had been doing for the past ten years? Would a true child of God even want to do those things? God is not the author of confusion, but confusion was running rampant through my aching heart and mind.

I didn't know where to turn for guidance. I knew only two Christians at the time, and I wasn't comfortable enough to go to either one of them. One was a neighbor of mine, but I didn't know her well enough to pour my heart out to her. The other was the contractor Dan worked under, but I certainly didn't want *him* to know what kind of shape we were in. I had put my Bible away ten years earlier when I had walked out on God. In all of that time, I had not opened it once. God's Word never crossed my mind as a place to hear God's voice.

The contractor, Lyndon Terrell, was also Dan's best friend. Lyndon had recently been saved and called to preach, and he was eager to share his faith with us. One day he gave Dan a tape of one of their revival services to bring home to me. The evangelist was Ed Ballew, someone whom Lyndon knew I had always respected as a great man of God. I took the tape and placed it by my stereo. It lay there for two weeks before I popped it in the cassette player and listened.

This day had been a frustrating and stressful one for me. I was very sick, and the rest of my world was falling apart, too. Nothing was going right, and things weren't showing any signs of improvement! I was going through the motions of the day—miserable and hopeless. I wanted answers, but I didn't know were to find them. I knew the tape was there, but surely it didn't contain the answers that I needed. Desperation and frustration drove me to the tape in hopes of hearing God's Voice.

The title of the sermon was, *"Are You Going to Hell?"* Conviction tugged at my heart as I listened intently. This same evangelist had led me to the Lord when I was twelve years old, but since then I had strayed far away from God. Maybe I had just gone through the formalities of obtaining salvation without experiencing a true regeneration. Perhaps I *was* going to hell. I had to know for myself. After ten years of wondering, I knew it was time to open my Bible again.

I'd put it off as long as I could. Dan had come in from work, and the boys had come in from playing, and I had to be mother and wife now. I hardened my heart and made it through the evening.

After dinner I put the boys to bed. The day had taken its toll on me, and I was tired. I lay down to try and sleep. I wasn't there long before conviction gripped my heart—much stronger than before. I thought God had quit dealing with me for the day! He had tugged at my heart earlier, but now He had a *death grip* on it. I thought I was literally going to die. My back hurt, I had a headache, and I became sick at my stomach. I tried to get away from it, but the harder I ran the worse it got.

Dan could sense that something was wrong. I couldn't even understand the warfare going on inside myself, so there was no sense in trying to explain it to him. I told him that I just didn't feel well. He needed to rest, so I went to the living room to deal with my pain. I flung myself despairingly on the sofa, the message from the tape that afternoon lingering in my mind, and cried out to God.

"Am I going to hell?" I caught myself asking aloud. "God, help me! God, please help me." The pain and conviction had become much more than I could bear. "Who can I go to, Lord? Show me where I can go for answers." In that instant, the Lord drove me back to the Bible I had placed in a drawer so many years ago.

When I opened my Bible, God faithfully began to answer my questions. The first place He took me was to John 3:16: "For God so loved the world that he gave his only begotten Son, that whosoever believeth in Him should not perish but have everlasting life." He reminded me that He had died for *even me;* He loved me that much! Then He took me to a promise in Romans 10:9–13:

> That if thou shalt confess with thy mouth the Lord Jesus, and shalt believe in thine heart that God hath raised him from the dead, thou shalt be saved. For with the heart man believeth unto righteousness; and with the mouth confession is made unto salvation. For the scripture saith, Whosoever believeth on him shall not be ashamed. For there is no difference between the Jew and the Greek: for the same Lord over all is rich unto all that call upon him. For whosoever shall call upon the name of the Lord shall be saved.

I had highlighted those scriptures in my Bible fourteen years ago. Now God was using them—all these years later—to let me know that *I truly had* been born again at twelve years old. He brought it all back to me—just as I had experienced it that night. My salvation hadn't been an emotional decision; I had truly experienced God's life-giving power. Yes, I was one of His own!

The Love Affair

Still, I had questions for Him, and that's where *the love affair* began. Dan would prop me up in my bed or on the couch, and I would read the Word of God for four to six hours a day. My seizures were so frequent and uncontrollable that I wasn't able to do much of anything else. The more I studied His Word, the more I came to know God personally. And the more I learned about Him and His love for me, the closer I drew to Him and the more intimate we became.

The next thing I knew I had fallen passionately in love with Jesus, the Savior of my soul. Through my readings, I'd recently learned that it was OK to question God—as long as I also gave Him an opportunity to answer my questions. He showed me examples in His Word of times when Moses, David, and other great biblical people had questioned Him, and He explained how He had answered *their* questions. With childlike faith, I decided to question God about my own life, going straight to His Word for answers.

First, I asked God why I was having all these problems in my life. He answered me out of Revelation 2:4: "Nevertheless I have somewhat against thee, because thou hast left thy first love." It seemed that God was telling me that He had *"somewhat"* against me, too, because I had left my first love. Somehow, this didn't surprise me, since I knew deep down inside that I *had* done just that!

Now that I knew that God had something against me, what I wanted to know is whether He hated me for it. In my mind, that's exactly what I thought—that God must hate me. Why else would

He allow all of this disaster in my life? I found the answer to these questions in Hebrews 12:5–7:

> And ye have forgotten the exhortation which speaketh unto you as unto children, My son, despise not thou the chastening of the Lord, nor faint when thou art rebuked of him: For whom the Lord loveth he chasteneth, and scourgeth every son whom he receiveth. If ye endure chastening, God dealeth with you as with sons; for what son is he whom the father chasteneth not?

Wow! It seemed clear that through my adversities God was letting me know that He loved me and He wouldn't let me walk away from Him without taking a hand of correction to me. Oh, I see. *Tough love* again . . . like Dolly's. But I found that hard to believe. Knowing my own faults and failures all too well, I just couldn't understand how He could love something like me.

I certainly wasn't Christian material. I had made too many mistakes and committed too many sins. How could I receive God's love and forgiveness? I asked God these questions, and once again He answered from the written Word:

> But if we walk in the light, as He is in the light, we have fellowship one with another, and the blood of Jesus Christ his Son cleanseth us from all sin. If we confess our sins, he is faithful and just to forgive us our sins, and to cleanse us from all unrighteousness. (1 John 1:7, 9)

Though I struggled with God in prayer for many hours on this issue, it was through the Spirit's revelation of the meaning of Jesus' life and the shedding of His blood that I was able to accept God's love and forgiveness by confessing my sins to Him. I guess people hear from God in different ways—through preaching, a witness, or sometimes His audible speaking Voice. For me, it was the Word of God which spoke to me, and it seemed in that hour to be a hand-delivered love letter written exclusively to me. The Bible's contents, once so dry and boring, seemed to take on a life of their own and dance across the table of my mind like the most colorful, thrilling stage production—inviting me to join in a love affair to remember!

I couldn't believe what I was hearing from the Word of God. I stood amazed by what God was telling me. I no longer viewed Him as a mean, evil, punishing God. It was clear now that He loved me in spite of my sins, my mistakes, and my failures. Oddly, I was even coming to realize that God was "loving" me through the seizures. He knew what circumstances it would take in my life to draw me closer to Himself. Through the seizures, He corrected my life and turned my attention to *the one and only* true God!

Going Backwards to Go Forward

Yes, I knew now that I was indeed a child of God. I had received Jesus as my Savior, but I had walked away from the Lord at sixteen years of age and wandered in Egypt for well over ten years. I had gotten so far out into the world, fleshly pleasures, and keeping up with worldly standards that I had literally smothered God's presence in my life with distractions. In fact, I had chosen *everything* in life that was the opposite of God's righteousness. Deceived by Satan, I had done a great job of deceiving myself, as well. By my own will, I had chosen a lifestyle that completely distracted me from God and any pursuit of righteousness. *How did I do this?*

My own particular brand of worldliness was based on my early love of country music. The sad lyrics in this musical style related to my life so well. I found comfort in knowing that some-one *else* was hurting, too. I immersed myself in every facet of this musical genre and, believe me, there was nothing about coun-try music that I didn't know.

Even my career was based on country music. I had been a dance teacher and choreographer since the age of twenty-one, and my career was pretty well established when I had my first sei-zure three years later. Naturally, the seizures hindered my work. Because the vibrations on my brain intensified the severity and frequency of seizures, the doctors ordered me to quit my job. But dance and country music controlled my life so strongly that I refused to give in. Unless I was literally unable to dance because of paralysis or illness, I continued right on doing it . . . Clearly, I had made country music my god. This went on for many years. Even after I started going back to church, I continued my dance-teaching career . . . until God convicted my heart.

In 1990, we were entering and winning dance competitions throughout the Southeast. I had over a hundred students in my dance classes when God suddenly took the desire to dance away from me.

One Sunday afternoon we had a dance competition nearby. I went to church that morning, and as soon as the service was over I headed for the competition. I was on stage in a mini-skirt danc-ing to country music when one of the groups from our church arrived to sing as part of the day's entertainment. Conviction hit me hard. Just a few short hours ago, these same people had seen me singing praises to God in the church choir. What would they think of my Christian character now? Mortified and deeply sorrowful, I never danced again after that day.

I went home convicted once again, but this time I knew that I had to give in to God. Dancing was not God's will for my life; it was something *I* wanted to do. That day I realized the true sinfulness of my career and lifestyle. Perhaps for others this might not represent so great a distraction, but I had fallen so deeply in love with Jesus that I didn't want *anything* to hinder our love affair. I had returned wholeheartedly to my first love—with the full intention never to stray from Him again.

Chapter 5

The Healing

The morning after my Sunday afternoon dance contest, I woke up hurting, unable to talk, and disfigured on the right side of my body. Debra brought medicine to my bedside and told me that I had been through several seizures the night before. Dan had gone to work, and she was going to stay with me until he came home.

One of the hardest things for me about the seizures was not being able to *do* anything. I hated being forced to lie in bed or on the couch all the time. It made me angry that I couldn't take care of myself and my family. Usually on days like that I would cry all day long. This particular morning was different.

Instead of crying I signaled for Debra to bring me my Bible. I had been experiencing a greater longing to know God's will for my life. Maybe I could find some direction in the Word today, if I could do nothing else.

I knew that God's Word would teach me not only about Himself, but about myself as well. If anywhere, it was here that I could find His purpose and plan for my life. As I opened the Bible that morning, I prayed for God to show me what He wanted me to do. God took me to Matthew 6:33: "But seek ye first the kingdom of God, and his righteousness; and all these things shall be added unto you."

"I don't know how to seek You first in my life, Lord," I thought prayerfully.

He took me to Hebrews 12:1:

Wherefore seeing we also are compassed about with so great a cloud of witnesses, let us lay aside every weight, and the sin which doth so easily beset us, and let us run with patience the race that is set before us.

I knew from that point on that God truly knew me better than I knew my own self. He knew my heart, and He was answering my questions before I even asked them! Somehow, the message hit me louder and more clearly than it ever had before that morning: I had to lay aside my sin and put *Him first.*

Truthfully, there was an abundance of sin in my life, and I had been hindered by it for many years. For years, I had been thinking that God was punishing me, but that "punishment," as I'd called it, was really the effects of my sin. What a revelation! Everything I'd experienced I had brought upon myself. The things I had angrily blamed God for were my own doing. My biggest problem was the life I had chosen to live, but God was faithful to show me the way of escape. His unconditional love, which poured in at the moment I acknowledged that these things were all too true, was totally overwhelming.

Since I had fallen passionately in love with my Lord and Savior, Jesus Christ, my problems didn't seem so great anymore. My dreams and desires were changing, too, from worldly to spiritual ones, and I longed to be more pleasing to God. Up to this point, my whole life had been centered on what *others* expected of me. I had focused on pleasing everyone around me, but now my desires and attention were focused on Christ. I knew that I had to do all I could to become more pleasing to Him.

Accepted in the Beloved

Dan and I joined a small Baptist church about twenty-five minutes from home. We found such peace, comfort, and contentment there. Dan and I also became very involved in the activities at our new church, as did the children. Dan taught the adult Sunday School class, and we both sang in the choir. We always looked forward to Sundays and Wednesdays, when we could fellowship with our church family.

Everyone at our new church fellowship was so loving and caring. There were many times when I would have a seizure right before the service, but Dan would dress me and take me to church anyway. He would have to carry me in and set me on a pew. Though I was unable to carry my own body, I had a great desire to be in the house of God with His people. At this point, Dan and I had *both* fallen in love with God, and we were determined not to be defeated by our circumstances.

Being in church with God's people was a great comfort for us all. We found church to be a resting place, but God was also using us in a unique way there. One particular evening, I had been through a series of seizures before church. Curled up immobile in my church pew, someone came by and hugged me. They confessed to me that they had not wanted to come to church because they'd had a headache, but seeing me sitting there paralyzed and disfigured had reminded them to be thankful and persevering. Their headache didn't seem so great anymore.

We never knew until that night that our continuing battle with seizures could have a positive effect on someone else's life. What we had been calling negative and hopeless, God was using as a positive in the lives of others. In this and other ways, the Lord encouraged Dan and I to keep on in the new direction He had shown us—and gave us joy in the midst of sorrows.

To Obey Is Better than Sacrifice

There wasn't much that I was able to do most of the time, so I read and studied my Bible for hours every day. The seizures left me speechless and without memory of key people and events in my life. Unable to do anything else, I would turn to God's Word. I found comfort in the pages of my Bible. Actually, it amazed those around me that I was able to read and understand God's Word. I couldn't walk, or talk, or even remember my family, but I didn't have any trouble comprehending God's Word. This in itself seemed miraculous!

I would get so excited over the small but wondrous thing the Lord would teach me about Himself. I couldn't wait to get my speech back to share it with somebody else! When I did, I would tell *everybody* what the Lord had shown me. Humbled and grateful, I just couldn't believe that he would speak personally to someone like me.

It was hard to keep those things to myself. Paralyzed and without speech, I would lie in bed praying for God to make me able to talk—just so I could share what I had learned from His Word with someone else. It wouldn't be long until my voice would return, and I would start in telling folks about what I had just learned in the Scripture.

It seemed that every time I opened my Bible God kept drawing me to the book of Daniel. This happened daily for over a year. I read Daniel over and over, verse by verse and chapter by chapter, but I couldn't understand why God kept taking me there. This was an Old Testament book of prophecy. What did God want me to see in it?

I grew so weary of reading Daniel that, in frustration, I finally asked the Lord what I had been missing. God drew me to the sixth chapter of Daniel, and I realized that He was leading me to *find a place* where I could be alone with Him to pray three times a day, as Daniel had. I questioned God's reasoning for that. *"Lord, can't you hear me wherever I pray?"* But God reminded me that *obedience is greater than sacrifice,* and I knew then what I had to do.

Dan had put a nice-sized walk-in closet in the bedroom of the home we had recently built, and I chose that as my place to be alone with God. I prepared an altar in my *prayer closet,* and I would slip away privately and pray there three times a day. Satan would often use the weakness of my flesh to try and hinder my obedience to God in this matter. Ever so slightly, he placed seeds of disobedience in my mind. *"Isn't this silly? You can pray anywhere; you don't have to do this."* The battle was difficult, particularly on days when I was barely able to walk, but I pushed those voices of discouragement out of my mind and went on with my prayer life.

My first prayer of the day was usually around 9:00 A.M. With Dan gone to work and the boys off to school, it was a great time to be alone with God and to get my day started on a positive note. This was my time of prayer for my family. I prayed for Dan, for our boys, and for myself. I prayed that God would strengthen each one of us in our walk with Him and that He would teach us His Word and His will for our lives. I prayed for His protection to surround us, and I asked Him to use everything about our lives, including the seizures, for His honor and glory. Then I'd go about my housework, errands, Bible study, and phone calls, as usual.

Around 12:30 in the afternoon I would go to my closet again. This time my prayers were specifically for the needs of others. I had a list of people to pray for, and it was always a pleasure to be able to add someone else to my list. And God was answering my prayers for others! At this second prayer time, I never prayed for myself, but each time I would head out of my closet I would say, *"Thank you, Lord, for healing me in your time and in your way, and until then use these seizures for your glory."*

Lessons in Prayer

At nine o'clock nightly, after the children were settled in bed, I would go back to my closet one last time—just to praise the Lord for the day. Regardless of what had happened that day, I found a reason to praise Him. If I had been through ten seizures or hadn't had one at all, I still praised Him just for giving me one more day with my family. Through this prayer, the Lord taught me to be content in whatsoever state I found myself. He had also taught me to rejoice in Him always. My prayer of praise every night brought me closer to Jesus, and I began to see Him working in every circumstance—good and bad. Truly, and for the first time in my life, I was learning to rejoice in all things.

There were many, many times when the seizures made me unable even to *walk* to my prayer closet. My right side would be completely paralyzed, so I would pull myself onto the floor and use the left side of my body to drag myself down the hallway to my little altar—just to offer God my praises. Dan would volunteer to carry me in there, but I knew I had to do this on my own. It was something very personal between me and God.

I continued praying three times a day, every day, for three years. If by chance I was not at home at one of my prayer times, I would find somewhere to slip away and pray. The Holy Spirit was faithful to remind me of my prayer time, and I would always find somewhere to meet with God when the time came. I once prayed in the bathroom stall of a shopping mall! In any case, I always found a place to kneel and pray.

My prayer life had become an essential part of my personal walk with God. It had drawn me closer to the Lord because I had learned to communicate with Him about *everything*. One thing I grew to realize was that my prayers were *not* a way of keeping *God informed* about my life. By praying, I wasn't telling *Him* anything that He didn't already know, but I sure was learning a great deal about myself. In fact, God was using my prayer life to teach me who I was in Him. My prayer life also taught me how to listen for His voice. Surprisingly, I found out that prayer is the essential ingredient to a personal, unhindered relationship with Christ.

A New Song

I had been praying daily for two years when I felt God calling me to sing. I fought God for over two weeks on that one! I was sure that either I was misunderstanding Him or He had made a mistake. I told Him that I couldn't sing because I had seizures, and that seizing paralyzed my speech. He reminded me that He already knew *that*. But I still had another excuse.

I told God that I just flat wasn't good enough to sing for Him. Sure, I could sing in the choir; there were plenty of other voices there to drown mine out. I reminded Him that I had never had a singing lesson in my life, so there was no way I could sing by myself. I suggested to God that He needed to leave that kind of singing to the professionals. The effects of my disobedience in this area were soon clear to me.

My prayer life was void and my Bible study time became dry and ineffective. Finally, unwilling to again be hindered by circumstances, I surrendered to God's will. I told Him that I would do whatever it took to make my prayer and study life effective again. Instantly, He reminded me that singing His praises publicly was the answer. Still, I was afraid.

"Lord, what if I have a seizure before I go on stage? What if it takes away my speech and I'm unable to sing? If that happens, we'll both look bad." And *those* were only the beginnings of my doubts and fears. *"Where will I sing? Who would want someone like me singing to them?"* I argued. Once again, God faithfully answered all of my questions.

In the book of Exodus, God showed me that Moses had had the same kinds of doubts and fears that I did. Moses didn't think that He was capable of doing what God had called him to do, either. So God sent Moses a mouthpiece in the form of his brother, Aaron. The story goes like this:

> And Moses said unto the Lord, O my Lord, I am not eloquent, neither heretofore, nor since thou hast spoken unto thy servant: but I am slow of speech, and of a slow tongue. And the Lord said unto him, Who hath made man's mouth? Or who maketh the dumb, or deaf, or the seeing, or the blind? Have not I the Lord? Now therefore go, and I will be with thy mouth, and teach thee what thou shalt say. (Exodus 4:10–12)

As I read about Moses' fear of public speaking and of God's solution to it, I knew that if God were truly calling me to sing for Him, He would be my mouthpiece, too. In His subtle way, God showed me that He would be with me as I stepped out in public ministry and that He would open all the doors He wanted me to walk through. I had no more excuses, so I did what I knew God wanted me to do.

Dan and I formed New Desire Christian Ministries in 1990. We began singing in our home church. Soon we were singing in other local churches, too. Before long we had covered the state of Georgia and were singing in churches throughout the Southeast. Today we travel across the United States and Canada in ministry for the Lord, and our music and literature has circled the globe for Christ. We get letters every day from people whose hearts have been touched and encouraged to hear what God has done for our family.

For over a year after we started singing I was still having seizures, but they never paralyzed my speech again. Sometimes I would have a seizure thirty minutes before going on stage, but it never affected my voice.

In the beginning, there were many times when Dan would have to carry me into a church to sing. He would sit me in a chair on the platform and hold my microphone while I sang because my right side was paralyzed, but God always gave me the strength and the voice to do His work. Often Dan would have to dress me, do my hair, and put on my make-up, but we were determined to do what God had called us to do. Amazingly, we never canceled even one appointment due to the seizures. God always made a way for us to be able to carry on.

The doors God opened for our singing ministry also increased my prayer ministry. Even though we were traveling to sing so often, my prayer life was still pretty well intact. I had grown to love God very deeply, and I depended on Him for everything. I had a hunger to love people with God's love and to give them hope for their lives. Inevitably, we always left a singing engagement with a list of names of people to be added to my prayer list. As I found my joy in praying for others, my own problems felt much less significant.

I always took the prayer requests of others very seriously. I sought God's Word on how to pray for each person's unique circumstances, and we saw many amazing answers. If God ever honored anything about my prayer life, it was most certainly my prayers for others.

"You can serve Me now."

On February 17, 1991 I was at home alone. Dan was at work, and the boys were at school. I was vacuuming the living room floor when the Holy Spirit reminded me that it was time for my 12:30 prayer for others. I stopped what I was doing and headed for the prayer closet in my bedroom. I took my prayer list and began to pray. When I finished, I started out the door and, as usual, I said, "Lord, thank You for healing me in Your time and in Your way. Until then, use my seizures for Thee."

I went back to the living room and resumed my vacuuming. Out of nowhere I heard someone say, "You're healed. You can serve Me now." The Voice was so real that I thought someone had come in the front door. I turned the vacuum cleaner off to see who it was, but there was no one there. I must have been imagining things. I remember saying to God, *"Lord, I want to be healed so bad so that I can serve You without hindrance. Please keep me patient and use me as You will until then."*

I turned the vacuum cleaner back on, and once again that same voice spoke: "The hindrance is gone. You're healed. You can serve Me now." This time I knew I was hearing the Voice of God.

When I realized what was going on I was back in my room, kneeling beside my bed. I was shouting praises to God because I knew my healing had come! The phone rang, and when I picked it up I heard Dolly say on the other end; "Brenda, are you all right up there? The neighbors heard you shouting, and they thought you might be having a seizure." I said, "No, Dolly, I'm fine. I'm just having a Holy Ghost spell, and I'll have to call you back."

When I hung up the phone I shouted for a while. After that I sang for a while, then I laughed and cried for a while. I was truly rejoicing in the Lord because the Great Physician had healed my life.

". . . Nothing Wavering . . ."

For two months after my healing, God wouldn't let me tell anyone, not even my mother, that it had happened. I wanted so badly to tell her, and one day I questioned the Lord about why I couldn't. In the book of James, chapter one, He showed me the following scripture:

> If any of you lack wisdom, let him ask of God, that giveth to all men liberally, and upbraideth not; and it shall be given him. But let him ask in faith, nothing wavering. For he that wavereth is like a wave of the sea driven with the wind and tossed. For let not that man think that he shall receive anything of the Lord. (James 1:5–7)

Through this verse, the Lord showed me that I still had a *trace of doubt* in my heart that He had actually healed me. I had to confess to him that He was right. So I asked the Lord to turn me from my doubt, and I promised *never* to question His healing power in my life again. In a bold act of faith, I went into the living room and turned on the ceiling fan. I knew that if anything could cause me to have a seizure, this would do it. If I had truly been healed, its rotation would have no effect on me. So, I sat watching the ceiling fan revolve for forty-five minutes! Incredibly, I never had the slightest hint of a seizure. There was no doubt left in my mind that God had healed me of epileptic seizures.

Immediately I ran down the road to Dolly's. Dan was at work, and I just had to tell *somebody* what God had done. I ran to my mother's bedroom and called through the window to Dolly. "I've got something to tell you," I said.

"We know," they replied. Well, I wanted to know just what they *thought* they knew. "God's healed you," Dolly said. That spoiled all the fun! How had they found out when I hadn't told anyone? "Brenda, you haven't had a seizure in two months," said Dolly. "We haven't had to feed you, bathe you, or take care of you at all for two whole months."

I had gotten so excited about being healed that I'd actually forgotten that it had been so long since I'd had a seizure. When Dan got home I could hardly wait to tell him, but I wanted to do it at the right time. After dinner he sat down in his recliner, and I sat down on the arm of his chair. "Honey, the Lord has healed us," I said. "I hope He has," he replied nonchalantly. I was almost upset by his indifference, but I knew that he had been through so much in the past six years that I really couldn't blame him for his skepticism. I knew that God would reveal His miraculous healing work in me to Dan soon.

I was sweeping the kitchen floor around lunchtime the next day when I heard Dan come speeding into the driveway. I stepped out onto the deck to see what was going on. The look on his face didn't show fear or worry, and my heart leaped as I knew that God had opened his eyes to the healing. My husband ran up the steps and embraced me in His arms. With tears of joy he said, "God spoke to me on my job today, honey. *We're healed!*"

To my joy, yesterday's indifference had been replaced by enthusiasm. What I'd tried to tell him the day before, God had revealed to Him that day. Left speechless by God's grace, we stood there embracing one another as we rejoiced in a cascade of tears.

Hurting to Be Healed

In just a few short years, our whole lives had been changed. Six years earlier, we were living in unrighteousness and sin. Then, we had found our pleasures in the things of the world. We desired worldly increase, and God was far from our minds. But with compassion, God had stepped in with a *tough love* solution and brought us right back to Himself. He removed our desire for the material and temporary things of this world and replaced them with *a new desire,* a desire to serve God wholeheartedly.

Chapter 6

A New Beginning

fter the Lord healed me and stopped the seizures, our lives changed dramatically. We knew, of course, that only God could have performed such a miracle. The doctors could not believe that my sickness had just *vanished*. But even the *symptoms* were gone! The piercing headaches, the aura, the dizziness, the blurred vision, all of it just *went away* from that moment in my living room on.

A year before I was healed, I had taken myself completely off of medication. *Though I don't recommend this to anyone without their doctor's approval,* the prescriptions I was taking, due to their many side effects, only seemed to be making my problems worse.

In five short years I had been on more than twenty different anticonvulsants. The doctors had prescribed medications for my nerves, my back problems, to help me sleep, and so on. I felt like a walking pharmacy! Honestly, if I had taken everything that had been prescribed for me at the same time, I would have overdosed. Now, all of that was over.

Never again would I have to worry about the medications or their side effects—because my seizures were *gone!* At last, after six grueling years, Dan and I had been both *physically and spiritually* healed. We knew that there would still be great hurdles to jump, but our faith was in God. We had come this far through Him, and with God's help we experienced renewed faith that we could overcome any battle that lay ahead.

A New Desire

Our *old desire* to survive and conquer life had also been renewed by the Lord. Now our greatest desire was to share what God had done for us with others. Dan and I *both* were overwhelmed with an excitement and passion to give God's love and hope to others who were facing catastrophic circumstances. We knew that if God could and would heal us, then He would do so for other men and women like ourselves, also.

We were now totally sold out to Jesus, and He had given us a testimony that could reach out and give even the most defeated person hope. Still, we didn't want to give anyone a false hope, so we carefully sought the Lord as to how He would have us share what He had done in our lives.

Dan and I knew of too many hurting people searching for answers who were deceived and led astray by man-made doctrines and *"Name it and Claim it"* religion. Together we prayed that God would show us the right way to share our miracle with others. We wanted especially to be used of Him in a way that *He* would be magnified through all. We wanted to see lives changed for Christ's sake. Through our own experience, we'd learned that God has the answer to every question and the solution to every problem. Our *new desire* was to share this fact with the whole world.

Throughout the last few years of my illness I had grown exceptionally in the knowledge and wisdom of God's Word. I had read the Bible through nearly eleven times over a period of four years. By the power of the Holy Spirit, the meat of God's Word had been taught to me, and I was eager to share what I had learned with others.

I had learned truths about God that no man could teach me, and these truths had made me free inwardly. I no longer feared dying and going to hell. I *knew* that I had to confess my sins daily to God and turn to Him for the power to overcome them.

I now believe that God's purpose for the seizures was to bring me to this exact point. He put me in a situation where I had nowhere to turn but to Him, and where I was unable to do anything *but* that. My years of prayer and study had prepared me for God's calling on my life. I realized now what I had to do. God was calling me to sing, to share my testimony, and to teach His Word to my fellow women.

Still, I struggled with this calling for a long time. I couldn't understand why God would call me to do these things when I had never been the type of person who liked to stand in front of a crowd. I had been quiet and withdrawn for most of my life. Because we were poor and were made fun of as children, I was intimidated by people and crowds. I had a *serious* inferiority complex and I felt out of place in large crowds of people. Truthfully, I couldn't imagine trying to share my testimony with others.

My appearance was also one of my greatest reservations. I was very self-conscious about it. I was 5'5", and I weighed only about 98 pounds. Dan often told me that the wind would blow me away if I didn't gain some weight.

I couldn't gain any weight because my seizures were so hard they kept it off. Every time I would stand to sing or to share my testimony, Satan would tell me that *I was ugly* and that people weren't paying any attention to what I was saying because they were too busy looking at how ugly I was. I recognized that hindrance as the voice of Satan and I pushed it to the back of my mind. My next problem was not so easy to deal with, however.

Called to Teach?

I was born a sinner, but I was raised a Baptist. I was taught that women had no right to speak, to pray, or to testify out loud in church. I wondered how people were going to accept me sharing my testimony at the pulpit. I prayed for God to show me His mind on this matter because I was very strict on myself when it came to talking in church. I didn't want to usurp authority over any man, and I certainly didn't want to be unscriptural in responding to what it seemed clear that God had called me to do. But, as always, the Lord freed me from bondage to these fears through His Word.

In Galatians 1:10 He said, "For do I now persuade men, or God? Or do I seek to please men? For if I yet pleased men, I should not be the servant of Christ." When I read this verse, I knew that God was reminding me I could not frustrate myself worrying about what man would think. I had to concentrate on pleasing and obeying God. He reminded me of where He had brought me from and of what I had to do in response to all He'd done for me.

He said in Psalm 150:6, "Let every thing that hath breath praise the Lord. Praise ye the Lord." I knew I had to praise God for His mighty presence in my life *unashamedly* and without reservation. Finally, God sealed my calling to service for Him with the instruction in Titus 2:3–5:

> The aged women likewise, that they be in behavior as becometh holiness, not false accusers, not given to much wine, teachers of good things; That they may teach the young women to be sober, to love their husbands, to love their children, to be discreet, chaste, keepers at home, good, obedient to their own husbands, that the word of God be not blasphemed.

From this point onward I left my fears and reservations with God. I went on by faith as God opened doors. I strived to serve God with the determination not to be hindered by man's opinions, judgments, or interpretations of my ministry. Truthfully, I faced many challenges in my service, especially when I started teaching women.

God had shown me that all my years of study had prepared me to be used for other women to be taught in and to grow in His Word. I could see that women everywhere were facing the same mental, spiritual, and emotional battles that I had faced. I had learned to turn to God and to allow Him to show me a way of escape, and this equipped me to teach others how to do so.

Most women don't live in that kind of freedom. Women face many fears because they are sensitive and intuitively see problems that may develop in a given situation. Incredibly, God had chosen *me* to show them how to give their problems to Him. Women today live in too much unnecessary shame, guilt, and bondage to fear—afraid that if they open up to someone else, their problem will be turned into the latest gossip. I'm sure I felt the same way myself once, but God showed me through my illness how "all things work together for good to them that love God, to them who are the called according to His purpose" (Romans 8:28). I learned to share everything with others, in hopes that God would get the honor and glory for what He'd done. Now, it seemed, our loving Father in heaven had appointed me to share the truth about His love with other women.

Although I felt certain that my ministry to women had been designed by God, I still faced many challenges. At times, I have been accused of being a "woman preacher," and of usurping authority over men. I've also been told that God couldn't use someone like me. I've even been told that my service is *way out of line.*" However, some of the same people who've made such accusations in the past now call me for prayer when they get into a bind. I know that my place is to serve God humbly—whether I am praised, blamed, questioned, or applauded for it—so that is what I strive daily to do.

Except for my ladies' meetings, Dan is on the platform with me wherever I go. He is a strict evangelist, and he knows the Scripture very well. As my headship, Dan makes sure that my words stay in line with God's principles in representing our ministry, and we always strive to follow the leadership of the Lord. Sometimes it's truly difficult to follow God's leadership—especially when man has programmed Him right out of the service (which is the case sometimes)! Sadly, we have learned that pleasing God does not *always* please man. And because we don't like to offend anyone, it *does* get stressful at times.

"Let This Mind Be in You . . ."

As I began to step out in ministry, I had to examine my own heart, attitude, and motivation according to the standards set in Philippians 2:5–8: "Let this mind be in you, which was also in Christ Jesus: Who . . . made himself of no reputation, and took upon him the form of a servant . . . and . . . humbled himself." In doing so, prayerfully, I came to some simple conclusions.

My greatest desire is to be a servant to the Lord. I truly want to serve others with God's love. I love people, and want them to know God personally and intimately. I want to teach people that *Jesus* is their only source of power. I don't want anyone to have to go through what we did in order to see God's authority exercised in their lives (though I realize that many will.)

I don't want people to doubt their salvation or to see God as cruel and punishing. God doesn't punish His children; He corrects them, and there is a big difference between the two. At Calvary, Jesus took upon Himself our punishment so that we might "come boldly unto the throne of grace, that we may obtain mercy, and find grace to help in time of need" (Hebrews 4:16).

When at last I understood this, and comprehended just how greatly God loves people, I was given a new love for others. Now I wish everyone could open up my heart and see the love I have for people. Because "God is love" (I John 4:7), I even love strangers— and I long to serve *everyone* with His love.

"A New Song Will I Give You . . ."

Initially, Dan and I had no *idea* how far God would take us in our service for Him. We have been singing as a family quartet for over ten years now. Dan and Labron *both* preach, and I write most of the songs we sing. I teach several different Bible classes, based on books that I have written, to ladies' groups in churches nationwide. I teach and sing at women's conferences and prayer retreats all across the country. We have seen countless souls saved through the ministry of New Desire each year, and it's all because of Jesus!

We can take no credit for any of this, for all the glory truly belongs to God. As a family, we are just honored that Christ Jesus allows us to work for His kingdom, and we are thankful that He knows our hearts and our deepest desires.

At long last, I can say that I am thankful for the seizures and all the mistakes I have made in my life. They were the *lovingly tough* lessons that led me back to close relationship with Jesus. Without them, where would I be? Yes, God knew what it would take in my life to cause me to surrender to Him, and He permitted them in my life accordingly. I now use all of my sins, mistakes, and failures for Him. With joy in my heart and a "tried and true," genuine hope for others, I share God's love everywhere I go.

Ain't God Good?

God is my life. He is all I have to offer to others, but He's also *all they need.* My life, my home, and my family are living proof of that! God is first in my life, even above Dan, my children, and my own pleasures. I have learned that if I put Him first in everything, the rest of life will fall into proper place. We are a family who loves God—not for what He has done for us, but simply because *first,* He loved us. Each of us longs to serve Him wholeheartedly.

God has taken a family that was broken and defeated and used us as an example of His divine love and grace. He has delivered us from all of our fears and has established us in His Word. We stand on His promises daily. We don't look back at our past and pity ourselves. When we do look back, it is to remind ourselves of how far God has brought us.

God has delivered us from the great financial burden that the ravages of my epilepsy had brought upon us. In fact, as I write this book, we have gone from over $100,000 in medical bills to all our bills being "PAID IN FULL." *Ain't God good?* We are so excited and grateful to be free from these debts at last!

What is the secret to financial freedom? I believe that God honors it when you do the best you can. Even in the worst of times, we didn't give up financially. We paid five dollars here and five dollars there (which was less than the full payment due), but at least we were putting forth an effort. It has taken us fourteen years to get back on our feet financially, but by the grace of God and through His mighty provision we now walk on level ground financially.

I have asked God, *"Why me? With so many people suffering, why did You choose to heal me?"* And while the reason *why* He chose to heal me is beyond my comprehension, I sure am glad that He did!

God gave me a new start, a new beginning in Him. I wasn't worthy of His love or of His healing power, but He taught me that *because of Calvary* and the shed blood of Jesus, I had been made worthy of healing, grace, new life on earth and eternity in heaven.

My goal now is to teach God's unconditional love everywhere I go. People need to know that *through Jesus Christ* they have been made worthy and that, *in Him,* old things have passed away, and all things have become new.

My message is also that, as children of God, our lives and our desires are made "new every morning" (Lamentations 3:23), so we must never dwell on the past. *God* doesn't dwell on our past; so we, too, must find the grace through Him to move beyond it and go on in life.

Chapter 7

Search and Seizure

*W*hen I had my first seizure in 1985, I had no idea what lay in store for me, what God was doing, or why. Sometimes it's best that way, I guess, or we'd never have the courage to make it. I had been raised not to question God, so I searched for answers in all the wrong places. My search put me through many trials and tribulations but, as they forced me to mature in the Lord I learned from them.

My search is now over! Now I know that God *used* the seizures to seize my life in a number of amazing ways. When I was yet in sin and disobedience, God reached down His hand and took hold of my life. And He hasn't let go since! I know now that *He never will.*

At Debra's house on that first day when the seizures began, I'd immediately imagined that they were some kind of judgment from God. I was bitter and angry with Him for it, too! Looking back now, I understand how Job must have felt at the end of his long trial. Job didn't understand his situation either, but once it was over he saw God in a new light and said:

> Who is he that hideth counsel without knowledge? therefore have I uttered that I understood not; things too wonderful for me, which I knew not. Hear, I beseech thee, and I will speak: I will demand of thee, and declare thou unto me. I have heard of thee by the hearing of the ear: but now **mine eye seeth thee.** (Job 42:3–5)

What Job once viewed as tragic and devastating he now called *wonderful*. God had seized *my life* just as He had Job's, and now my *eye had truly seen* the God I'd searched for so many years. I, too, could say that what I once viewed as tragic and devastating was honestly too wonderful for me to understand. *I just love Jesus!* Don't you?

A Grain of Faith

Even before I was healed of the seizures, our family saw God work in mighty ways. Once we surrendered our lives to Him, every day was filled with anticipation. It was exciting to see the Lord working in every area of our lives. Experiencing God's presence, power, and provision in a personal way is breathtaking and humbling every time, but there have been several times when it was absolutely frightening! I truly came to understand why people often say, "You'd better be careful what you pray for." It was *awesome* to me to see the surprising ways in which God often answered our prayers.

I surrendered to the Lord several months before Dan did. When I first started attending church, Dan wouldn't go with me. He never hindered the boys and me from going, but at the time he just didn't want any part of the Christian life. However, with my seizure disorder, he did worry about me driving. Except to go to church, I didn't drive unless I absolutely had to—and God was always faithful to protect me when I did.

Every time I started off to church I would pray that God would keep me from having any seizures. He heard and answered those prayers each time. In fact, I never had to worry when I got behind the wheel of the car to go to church. I knew that God had His hand on my life, and the hunger and thirst that I had to learn more about and to worship Him was the unstoppable force that activated my faith in God.

In my newly committed walk with God, I had acquired just enough faith in Him to believe that He would protect me and my children from an accident on our way to church. Amazingly, God used this tiny grain of faith to touch Dan's heart, also.

Dan was always waiting for us when we came home from church. And as soon as we would walk through the door, the look of worry on his face would change to relief. Immediately I would remind him that God had driven us to church and back, and God used those words to convict Dan's heart. Dan knew that only God could be doing this. Somehow when you see God work in such miraculous ways, you cannot deny His authority. Dan could not deny the protective care of God on us, so he learned not to worry . . . and began thinking more about this Loving Father who could do something he couldn't: hold back my seizures.

Meanwhile, Dan also witnessed a complete mental change in his wife. From three years of wrenching seizures, I had become physically and mentally drained. As noted, I had fallen into a deep depression. In fact, the presence of any real happiness in my life seemed very doubtful, especially to Dan. Now, day by day, he was watching God transform my life from one of doom and depression into a life of hope and joy.

I soon had no time or room within me for defeat. God had given me a new start in Him, and for me it felt like life had just begun. As I studied, prayed, and attended church, Dan witnessed me visibly transform into a new personality. In the Lord, I became happy, peaceful, and self-controlled. I no longer fell apart over every little adversity in our lives, and I even learned to stand strong in the greater tragedies that came our way.

I learned to trust God for everything. My usual voice of negativity was replaced by one of optimism about even the toughest issues in our lives. Dan knew that only God could have made *that* kind of difference in me, and the changes in me began to change him, too. Soon I no longer had to drive to church. Dan started going with us, and he did the driving! In His own mysterious and wonderful way, God had touched Dan's heart, and he, too, came to the place where he gave up his old desires and *sold out to the Lord.*

Seized by God

In the next couple of years, as we walked with Christ daily, our entire home was transformed. Our children changed from nervous and restless youth to calm and peaceful ones. They sensed the transformation throughout our household, and they, too, credited God.

They would go to school and tell their teachers and friends that we loved Jesus. We would all sit around the living room together talking about God and His Word, and the boys always listened carefully to each word.

Although Mother had raised us to go to church, neither my brother nor any of my sisters was in church when I started having seizures. Because she had no one to take her, Mother wasn't even able to go. Just as I had done, they had all strayed out into the world. As God transformed my life, my brothers and sisters, too, noticed the changes. I often invited them to church with me, but they refused every time. Then, one by one, God began working in their lives.

Debra, Dolly, and Mother started going to church with us. Soon, Debra's husband Lemuel was saved. They had all seen the presence and power of God at work in a very hopeless situation. You see, when God begins to work in one life, it has a domino effect in the lives of others. We became witnesses to everyone with whom we came into contact, whether family, friends, or strangers. And everyone who had daily contact with us was affected by the almighty power of God.

Things happened every day that normally caused us setbacks, but God always provided us with the stability to face them. Never again did He allow us to be pulled back into a state of defeat. In difficulties, He faithfully sent encouragement and promises that we could cling to. Those around us would watch silently as God came through again and again, and they'd leave with a renewed hope in life for their own situation.

One particular occasion that Debra and Dolly often recall when talking about the seizures is a night that I have no recollection of to this day. According to them, a young lady came by my house for some scriptural counsel. While she was there, I had several *petit mal* seizures. During the seizures, I began to quote the book of Exodus, moving chapter to chapter, and then I told them what each chapter meant!

Dolly says that the young lady was amazed by what she heard. She said it was enough to make her surrender her life to God forever, and she did just that. Today this young lady will tell you that her whole perception of God changed that night. Yet I know that only God could have placed her in my home that evening, speaking to her the exact words that she needed. I don't recall any of it, but I am glad that God used my words for His honor and glory. And I'd gladly go through the agony of my seizures all over again just to see one soul draw nigh to God.

Since giving my life to God I had prayed daily that He would do whatever it took to bring my whole family into His righteousness. By now, I had given my illness and everything I had over to Him for His Kingdom use. I wanted the Lord to receive honor and glory from all of it. I had given God total control of my future, yet my flesh often feared what I might be praying for—until God's Spirit within me would remove my doubts.

When I felt fearful, He would remind me of 2 Timothy 1:7: "For God hath not given us the spirit of fear; but of power, and of love, and of a sound mind." Staying my mind on Christ, I could then dwell in perfect peace (Isaiah 26:3). In the next ten years as God worked in *fearful* but most wonderful ways, I saw many family members turn to the Lord for salvation.

In fact, God has shown Himself to us in so *many* ways that it would take a thick catalog even to list them all! Even now, He continues to work in amazing ways in our ministry, our family, and our personal lives each day. Throughout the years, we have learned that God cares about even the most minute details of our lives. Daily, He has revealed Himself in even the small, seemingly unimportant things.

The Bible teaches in Psalm 37:4 that, if we delight in Him, God will even give us the desires of our hearts. He does that faithfully for us, and He will for you, also.

Picture This

Probably one of the most trivial things I remember God doing for us is making it possible to have our picture in the church directory. In my illness, I was not allowed to have portraits made because the flash could easily trigger a seizure, but it meant so much to me for our family to be included in this book. We were in church and "on fire for God," and I desperately wanted our picture to be in the directory.

Dan wouldn't even consider it. He said that there was no sense in adding to our problems now. I begged and pleaded, but he wouldn't give in, so I turned my request over to God. I didn't mention it to Dan anymore, but prayed diligently for God to give him a peace that we could have our portrait done without my having a seizure. I had the faith to believe that God was hearing my prayers, too. So, one afternoon after I'd knelt by my bed and prayed specifically for this one request, I went to the closet and picked the dress I was going to wear in our portrait!

God had given me a peace about the situation, and I knew that He would give me the desires of my heart. Still, I didn't mention it to Dan. Three days later, he came in from work and told me that we were going to be in the church directory! He reported that God had spoken to him, and he now knew that it would be OK. Two weeks later we had our picture made, and I didn't have a seizure! Only God could have done that. It was just a trivial matter, but it was important to me, and God gave me the desire of my heart. *Ain't God good?*

I remember also a *major* incident where God worked in our lives. It was on a Sunday in December when I was still having seizures. I got up to get the boys ready for church that morning. I went into the living room and turned on the heater, but it wouldn't light. I quickly realized that we were out of fuel.

Dan's construction work had been slow, and most of the money he brought in had to be used for medicine and groceries. We had been so stressed out over bills that we forgot to order propane for the tank. We had only three dollars in cash, our checking account had been drained, and back then we didn't even *know* what a savings account was! Our pride was too great to tell anyone that we were hurting, and we had no idea what we were going to do.

We finished getting ready and headed to church. On the way, Dan said, "Honey, we don't have enough gas in the truck to get back home. What are we going to do?"

"We're going to have faith in God," I said. I knew we were going to Debra's for lunch after church that morning, and we planned to stay with her until the time came for the evening service. So, God had already made provision for our food. I knew He would take care of the rest. I gave our last three dollars to Dan and the boys for their Sunday school offering. We may have been in a tight spot, but Baptists always give a dollar in Sunday school!

By this time we had learned that we couldn't out-give God. After lunch at Debra's that day, we sat on the back steps wondering what we would do when the evening service was over. In our pride, we hadn't mentioned our need to anyone. That night we went to church, downhearted and doubtful, and prayed for God to make a way.

When the service was over, the family got up to leave. Then, just as I approached the door, a gentleman stopped me. He told me that he loved me and appreciated my teaching his teenage daughter about Jesus because she had almost given in to peer pressure, drugs, and alcohol until she started attending church. He said that he, too, would have died and gone to hell if I had not invited him to church and led him to the Lord. As he hugged my neck and shook my hand, I noticed that he left a small piece of paper in my palm. He told me not to read it until later, and he walked out the door and was gone.

Something told me to open it before I left because it would be too dark to read it in the truck. I was standing in the foyer, and Dan was just outside the door. I unfolded the paper, and it was a check for $500. Dan and I both ran out the door to catch the man before he left. When I caught up to him, I told him that we just couldn't take his money. He looked me in the eye and said, "It's not my money. It's God's money, and God told me today, standing in my kitchen after I ate lunch, to give you $500. If you don't take this money, you are turning God down."

With that, he got in his car and drove off. Absolutely no one knew about our financial condition, so only God could have impressed upon this man's heart to give a financial gift to us. God promises in His Word that *He will never leave us nor forsake us* and that He will supply all of our needs according to His riches in glory by Christ Jesus. God tested our faith that day and increased our trust in Him. He is *so real* in our lives.

We Walk by Faith, Not by Sight.

If I continued to tell you about the miracles God has performed in our lives, I could amaze you even more. For example, there was the time when God told me to give my car away. I didn't understand it at the time, but I knew God's Voice and I knew that I had heard it clearly. I gave the car to the person He told me to give it to, but I didn't know how I was going to get around without it! Then God sent me a newer car with fewer miles, and even provided the money to pay for it in full! Coincidentally, on the very morning I had called the lady to come get my car, the motor in the car she owned had blown up. Stories about God's great work in our lives could literally go on and on . . . but I'll stop here for the time being.

For years we have lived only by faith in Him. As a couple and as a family, we stand on the scripture that ". . . without faith it is impossible to please God" (Hebrews 11:6).

I have been healed from my seizures for eleven years now. Each day, I fall more in love with Jesus. For every morning that I get out of bed without anyone's help, I praise the Lord. I ask Him each day to let me shine for Him. Ecstatically, I thank Him that I can feed and bathe myself—and drive again. And the Lord has brought us *so* far, giving us a new desire to please Him. He has healed, delivered, and provided for us in such miraculous ways that those around us can only exclaim, "God alone could have done this."

Today, our family continues to minister in song and in the Word of God from church to church across the land. The following words are from a song that I wrote on one of those days when I just didn't feel worthy to be called God's servant. Circumstances in our lives, as they so often do, had gotten me down, but even in the midst of this God gave me a new song to sing for His glory.

I wrote "Underneath the Rubble" at 4:00 A.M. one morning as a personal hymn to Him. The verses are *what I said* to the Lord, and the chorus is *what He responded* to me out of the books of Psalms and Proverbs. I hope these lyrics will give you encouragement as you live for and love the Lord each day. God bless you as you do.

Underneath the Rubble

Underneath this fragile person, beneath the stress and agony,
There is a longing deep within me that sometimes it's hard to see.
Everybody really needs me; there's not enough of me to go around,
I want to live for Jesus, but circumstances hold me down.
Many times throughout the battle, when I think I've had enough,
I hear a still, small Voice within me saying, "Child, you can't give up."

Underneath all the rubble, there is a gem beyond compare.
You are a precious child to the Father; He knows everything you bear;
He understands all your weakness, your frustration, and your pain.
Lay it all at the feet of Jesus; God will use it for His gain.

So underneath all the rubble, you are a vessel of the Lord—
a very special person, on eagle's wings you can soar!

Today your heart is heavy; demands of life have drained you dry,
You wonder if others face this; are you the only one who cries?
You search to find the answers as you rummage through debris,
But underneath all your rubble, the Cross of Christ has made you free!

Ain't God good? I just love Jesus!

Chapter 8

But Until Then . . .

I don't have anything against *other* Bible versions; in fact,
I have studied from several of them, but I absolutely love
the King James Version of the Bible. The wording of the
King James—with its beauty and its strong presentation of the provision and power of God—fascinates me completely.

I especially cherish the words in Ephesians 3:20, which tell us
that God is able to do "exceeding abundantly above all that we ask
or think." God has certainly fulfilled this scripture in my life, in
my home, in my marriage, in my children and in my ministry. I
have truly witnessed His wonder-working power in every avenue
of my life.

I believe Ephesians 3:20 and cling to the promise it contains
every day. As I serve God now with a restored body and continu-
ally experience a deepening relationship with Christ, I suppose I
am living proof that He *will* do "exceeding abundantly above all
that we ask or think." In fact, by the grace of God, the six years I
spent in diligent Bible study during the "seizure years" that this

book has recounted eventually earned me something I'd always wanted: a doctorate degree in Divinity (D.D.) from Covington Theological Seminary in Rossville, Georgia. How I praise God for fulfilling the desire of my heart in this way.

Still, I've learned that complete holiness does not come without sacrifice and commitment. It does not come over night, nor does it guarantee that your life will be transformed into a bed of roses. In fact, our battles sometimes seem to become greater as we become more Christ-like. *Why?*

We all have an enemy. In fact, we have three! Our *enemies* are Satan, the world, and our own flesh. If we are not constantly on guard—and equipped with the full armor of God—then we will find ourselves totally deceived, devastated, and defeated.

On September 11, 2001, most of us found ourselves feeling deceived by our enemies, devastated by tragedy, and defeated in the flesh. We experienced fear, pain, and overwhelming turmoil within. We questioned God, pointed fingers of blame, and then wept as we witnessed the destruction of a city and the death of thousands of people from all nations.

This tragedy changed all of our lives forever and brought many of us back to the only One who can heal our hearts and our nation. Through this ruthless attack, God has been so faithful to comfort our hearts and to unite us as a nation. His Presence has been real through every phase of this devastating experience in our country, and each one of us alive that day will have a story to tell our children.

911: The Enemy Attacks!

I know how this day has affected *my* life. In fact, I will *never* forget September 11, 2001. For all of us, it started out as just another day of the week. I was at home, busily at work in our ministry office. The phone rang, and I heard my sister's voice on the other end—weeping uncontrollably about what she was seeing unfold right on her television screen. I ran to turn the TV on and to see what she was so upset about. The sight of the collapse of the second Twin Tower literally took my breath away! I started praying immediately for the thousands who would be affected by this senseless act of violence.

The enemy had caught us off guard and had succeeded in an apparent defeat. For the remainder of the week, our ministry phone lines were jammed with calls from people searching for answers to questions about this horrible attack. Strangely, I found myself reexamining my own life and reliving all the things that God had done and is still doing within me and for me.

Through this, I have realized that no work performed by God in a person's life should ever be permitted to grow stagnant. You see, around the same time of the World Trade Center attack, the enemy had caught me with my *own* guard down, as well. I had become unsure of God's concern for my ministry work and was having doubts about my service for Him. I had grown weak in my flesh and was experiencing burnout. And, once again, I was fighting physical battles on a daily basis.

Through my uncertainties and battles, the enemy was feeding me lies, and I was weak enough to believe them. Daily, he was growing more successful in convincing me that *God was through with me,* and that I was no longer effective in my ministry or as a Christian. It seemed he had almost convinced me that I no longer needed to publicly proclaim God's delivering and healing power in my life, and I began *ever-so-slightly* to pull back on God.

Satan tried to tell me that the healing of my seizures had become *old news,* and was no longer acknowledged by those I shared it with as God's Divine work. He also worked on my mind, convincing me that my past would always haunt me. I began to fear that my ministry would be destroyed because of man's backbiting and gossiping about my childhood, my broken marriage, and things that had happened in my life more than twenty years ago.

Through these mental onslaughts, I had grown steadily weaker in my service and in my relationship with Christ. The weaker I grew and the more doubt I experienced, the more I realized that only God could deliver me from such adversities. However, by His grace, God was faithful to revive and renew my spirit.

Counterattack: For His Glory

I began to call out to God in prayer and in fasting. I renewed my discipline in the study of His Word. I sought Him for instruction, and He was faithful to minister to me. He showed me what a counterfeit the enemy is and what I had to do to overcome my doubt and defeat. He was faithful to reaffirm His call upon my life. He reminded me that even though the seizures were old news, the message of my healing by God's grace was still effective for His glory today.

God also pressed upon my heart to share the tremendous work He has done in my life ever *since* the day I was healed of my seizures. Indeed, I have weathered many storms in my life since I first shared my life story publicly. Before September 11, 2001, I thought that these victories were minute and unimportant to everyone but me. However, as I watched the World Trade Center crumble to the ground—taking thousands of lives with it—I realized the importance of God's love for me. I realized my passion to share Him and the things He has done for me with others. I've realized through these past few years of trials that God still has a work for me to do until He calls me home, so until *then* my heart will go on singing and sharing the Gospel of Jesus Christ.

Storms, Battles, and Warfare

Since February 17, 1991 I have lived seizure-free. Today, February 28, 2002, I'm writing these words confined to complete bed rest by doctor's orders due to a severe bladder condition. Sometimes it seems the enemy's assaults against us never end, but neither do the gifts and calling of God.

Approximately ten months ago, I went to see my doctor for what I thought was a urinary tract infection. I drove myself to his office, but by the time I arrived, I was very flush and weak. The next thing I can recall is the sharp smell of an ammonia stick and being told I would be admitted to the hospital for further testing.

Because I fainted in his office, the doctor thought I might be having seizures again, but the test showed that I'd contracted an infection. A neurologist was called in to perform an MRI, an EEG, and a CT scan on my brain. The neurologist said he was *certain* that I was having mild to moderate seizures again.

Approximately one month before this, I had been in an auto accident. I was sitting still in traffic, waiting for a car to turn in front of me, when I was rear-ended by a man going nearly fifty-five miles per hour! This experience had left me with whiplash and two herniated discs in my neck. I was already being treated for these when I was hospitalized for the infection and for suspected seizure activity.

In my heart I knew that God was faithful to protect me from having seizures again. "God does not do anything *halfway*," I told myself and my family. I tried to explain this to the doctors, too, but they were determined to prove me wrong. So, I went through all the testing and stayed in the hospital four days longer.

For some reason, I was so dehydrated that my veins could not support the IV needles. The tests showed the urinary tract infection—and *some* abnormal neurological brain activity, but not *seizure activity*. The MRI revealed scarring on the upper left lobe of my brain and two herniated discs in my neck. It even pinpointed fluid build-up at the base of my brain, but showed absolutely *no* seizure activity. They could not understand or explain it, but I know why! One word says it all: *Jesus!* He is able to do *exceeding abundantly above* all that we can ask or think. Physical ills may slow me down someday, but until then I will carry on with God's calling!

Seeking the Healer

Each day, as I lay in the hospital suffering great pain, I found my strength in God's Word. I prayed without ceasing, living by faith that God would once again use my life as a testimony of His mercy, His grace, and His almighty power. It thrilled my heart to know that God was still at work in my life and that the Great Physician's Hand is the Divine Hand that keeps us from all harm.

I was discharged from the hospital with the diagnosis of an incurable bladder disease, which was causing my current problem. They scheduled me for treatments every two weeks for four months, and said that I would have to have maintenance treatments once a month *for the rest of my life* thereafter.

Due to the severity of my disease, these treatments are very painful. I cannot be sedated in any way at the time of the procedure. After the second treatment I learned that quoting Scripture and talking to God during the treatments makes them easier to handle. In other words, God is my strength and I know that He can get me through this, but I also know that *until He does* I will have to place all of my trust in Him.

My passion during this entire trial remains to see God use us in our ministry and for Him to expand our borders. One day, as discouragement threatened to overwhelm me once again, God showed me that my sickness was the hand of the enemy seeking to devour and hinder the good work of the Lord in our lives. His Spirit kept directing me to scriptures, such as 1 Peter 5:6–8:

> Humble yourselves therefore under the mighty hand of God, that He may exalt you in due time: Casting all your care upon him; for he careth for you. Be sober, be vigilant; because your adversary the devil, as a roaring lion, walketh about, seeking whom he may devour.

Now I know that we must recognize Satan's tactics so that we don't foolishly blame God when trials come our way. 1 Peter 4:12–13 says it this way:

> Beloved, think it not strange concerning the fiery trial which is to try you, as though some strange thing happened unto you: But rejoice, inasmuch as ye are partakers of Christ's sufferings; that, when his glory shall be revealed, ye may be glad also with exceeding joy.

These passages of Scripture became my very strength. They can become your strength, also, if your desire is for God to search and seize your life for His glory.

God has *searched and seized* every area of my life. For every adversity, His grace has been sufficient. Despite my sufferings, and the sufferings of others on my behalf, I have learned more about Him and grown closer to Him through it all. Now I can say that I truly understand why God allows the physical, financial, and daily battles of life. Without them, we would not *recognize* the love and compassion that He daily bestows upon us all.

The Bible says in 2 Chronicles 16:9, "For the eyes of the LORD run to and fro throughout the whole earth, to show himself strong in the behalf of *them* whose heart *is* perfect toward him."

I believe it is important that we do not teach *healing* before we teach God's *divine love and provision* for all who seek a relationship with Him. It is not always God's will for someone to be healed from physical adversity. In fact, I often wonder why He chose to heal *me*. I feel so unworthy, and I also know that there are so many others who need healing besides myself. But I suspect it has something to do with *seeking the Healer* and His will more than just seeking the healing, because that's what changed *my* life for the better.

I can honestly say that if God had never healed me of seizures, I would still serve Him. My relationship with God is not based on what He has *done* for me, but is based on His love for me. I never sought or focused solely on being healed. I focused on becoming pleasing to Him and being intimate with Him. It really didn't matter to me if I was healed or not. I knew that I loved Him and that He loved me, and I built on that. Even while I was still having severe seizures, I began to serve the Lord. Then one day I looked back and realized that God had taken care of the finances and removed the seizures. It was as simple as that.

The bladder disease I am now experiencing is another attack of the enemy in an attempt to hinder the work of the Lord, but I refuse to allow the devil to seize my love for God or my joy in His service. I know that this *too* shall work for my good, as all things do "to those who are the called according to His purpose." Just today, God reminded me of what Paul taught in 2 Corinthians 4:8–10:

> We are troubled on every side, yet not distressed; we are perplexed, but not in despair; Persecuted, but not forsaken; cast down, but not destroyed; Always bearing about in the body the dying of the Lord Jesus, that the life also of Jesus might be made manifest in our body.

The one thing I *have* learned is that God knows everything about me before it ever takes place. Therefore, I have accepted the truth that in my times of distress and perplexity, despair and persecution, God is preparing me to be used for His honor and glory, and until then I'll carry my cross.

I do not worry about tomorrow, nor do I fear the bladder disease, the neck injury, or the negative opinion of man. I praise God for *all* these things, for in them I know He will be manifested in my life.

I have learned that in Him I can do all things, and my desire is to deal with my adversities so that neither Satan, nor the world, nor the flesh can defeat me as a child of God. For so long I dwelt in my circumstances—and God could not deliver me because of my moaning and murmuring. His Word ministered to me on this issue, also, out of Philippians 2:13–16:

> For it is God which worketh in you both to will and to do of *his* good pleasure. Do all things without murmurings and disputings: That ye may be blameless and harmless, the sons of God, without rebuke, in the midst of a crooked and perverse nation, among whom ye shine as lights in the world; Holding forth the word of life; that I may rejoice in the day of Christ, that I have not run in vain, neither laboured in vain.

Pruning and Abundance

Through every obstacle I face, God is pruning my life with His skillful and loving Hand. He knows my heart and my sincerity. He searches my heart daily—not for His *own* understanding but for mine. God knows me better than I know myself. Therefore, His purpose for pruning my life is that I might confess (*admit*) and repent *(turn from sin, turning to God)* from all negative, sinful, and unwholesome issues within my life.

God longs to seize *(take possession of, capture, arrest)* everything about *you,* too, and to use it for the furtherance of His gospel. Your life is no different than mine. Perhaps you haven't had the problems that I've had, and perhaps you don't feel like your problems are as major as some of the ones I've described. It's also very possible that your adversities are a lot *greater* than mine. Regardless, God wants to possess them so that He can release you from them and use you for His honor and glory.

I believe that God's plan and purpose for our lives is a daily process. Holiness just doesn't happen over night. Yet we must be willing to serve Him regardless of our hardships. If He never chooses to heal us, we must serve Him. If He never chooses to free us financially, we must serve Him. If our marriage is never reconciled, we must serve Him. If we never overcome the mental and emotional battles we face, we must serve Him. Otherwise, we are guilty of serving our flesh and Satan has robbed us of the joy and peace that is ours through Christ. John 10:10 says, "The thief cometh not, but for to steal, and to kill, and to destroy: I am come that they might have life, and that they might have *it* more abundantly." Abundance, that is God's plan.

I'm so thankful that God has seized my whole life, both the positive and negative parts of it. I pray that something of what you've read here will challenge you to develop a deeper, more intimate relationship with our Lord and Savior, Jesus Christ. My life has always had obstacles, and yours will, too. However, for every obstacle God is our strength. Our job is to "press toward the mark for the prize of the high calling of God in Christ Jesus" (Philippians 3:14), and until I gain that prize, I'll carry on.

I praise God for everything I have gone through, and I wouldn't trade one moment of agony for all I've learned about the Lord through it. I would like to close with the lyrics of a song my husband Dan inspired me to write. When you feel defeated and ready to give up, as we *all* sometimes will, may it inspire you in some way to go forward, trusting His love.

I Wouldn't Change a Thing

I wouldn't change a thing,
for what I've learned about the Lord.
Every battle, every trial,
Has taught me more and more.
I would face another valley,
I would go an extra mile.
I would climb the highest mountain;
I would face another trial.
I wouldn't change a thing
for what I've learned about the Lord.
I've watched Him make provision,
And protect me from all harm.
I've found His grace sufficient,
when He held me in His arms.
I've wondered many times,
would tomorrow ever come?
Today looked mighty hopeless;
I felt that life was done.
I learned of His provision,

of His protection and of His grace.
I learned that on Golgotha,
Jesus took my place.
No, I wouldn't change a thing
for what I've learned about the Lord.

Brenda Robinson
Aragon, Georgia
2002

To order additional copies of

FOR HIS
GLORY

Have your credit card ready and call

Toll free: (877) 421-READ (7323)

or send $12.00* each plus $4.95 S&H** to

WinePress Publishing
PO Box 428
Enumclaw, WA 98022

www.winepresspub.com

*WA residents, add 8.4% sales tax

**add $1.00 S&H for each additional book ordered